THE BRITISH LIBRARY
writers' lives

William Shakespeare

Mr. WILLIAM
SHAKESPEARES

COMEDIES,
HISTORIES, &
TRAGEDIES.

Published according to the True Originall Copies.

Martin Droeshout sculpsit London.

LONDON
Printed by Isaac Iaggard, and Ed. Blount. 1623.

THE BRITISH LIBRARY
writers' lives

William Shakespeare

DOMINIC SHELLARD

OXFORD
UNIVERSITY PRESS

BRITANNIA

LO

S. Paules Church

THAMESIS

The Globe

Contents

≋ *Preface*

As of April 1998 the catalogue of the British Library listed 17,099 books devoted to some aspect of the career of William Shakespeare. The number probably increases every week. This compares with 958 for John Keats, 774 for Shakespeare's theatrical rival and friend, Ben Jonson, and 522 for his early competitor, Christopher Marlowe. There are several reasons for this phenomenal interest. Positive ones include the breadth of Shakespeare's intellect, the theatricality of his plays, the beauty of his poetry, the precision of his language and the perception of his insight. More questionable ones cover the self-perpetuating nature of the Shakespeare industry, the dominant position in the literary canon that successive generations of literary and dramatic critics have accorded him (to the possible exclusion of other valuable work) and the malleability of the Shakespeare icon to support various cultural or political causes (rather in the manner of the Bible). For, at the very least, Shakespeare possesses one of the most distinctive faces the world has ever witnessed. Everybody recognises the bald dome and the long hair over his ears. Such is the power of the Shakespeare brand that this face is seen at the end of the twentieth century as the very epitome of wisdom, even by those who would never dream of seeing a play of his in the theatre, let alone read one of his sonnets in the privacy of their own home. Or to be more accurate, the *artistic recreation* of his face as depicted in the Droeshout engraving that appears on the front of the First Folio (and the cover of this book) is seen as the epitome of wisdom. For even in our familiar visual image of Shakespeare, art merges with life, as with so much of his biography.

This brings us to another, often forgotten, reason for our fascination with Shakespeare, the fact that he is an enigma. Rather as with Jesus Christ, the usual facets of biographical accounts are irretrievably missing, such as what he liked to eat, or whether he was fond of ale or sack; did he actually know Queen Elizabeth, and why did his father suffer such a decline in fortune during his early childhood? This absence of hard fact (if such a thing can exist) has both enhanced his mystique and proved a huge source of frustration (spurring countless academics to scurry around Warwickshire in the hope of finding a crucial and priceless letter or manuscript that will fill in a gap or two). The aim of this book is not to conjure up ever-more speculation about his life from further re-analysis of some of the most over-analysed lines in literature. Instead it tries to marshal what we do know about Shakespeare's life into a fluent narrative to provide a context against which his literary output can be judged. In this, I hope it will demonstrate that we actually know slightly more about his existence than might be generally recognised.

In this task I have been guided by my own experience of teaching Shakespeare to undergraduates at the Universities of Salford and Sheffield, the research that I have conducted at the British Library and in Stratford and the invaluable scholarship of six of the 17,099 books cited above. I particularly wish to commend to those who would like to take this subject further the magnificent works by Stanley Wells, Eric Sams, Peter Thomson and S. Schoenbaum that I have listed in my section on Further Reading. They are as sure a guide as any through the most complex literary minefield of them all.

≈ *Acknowledgements*

I would like to thank several people for their friendship and encouragement during the writing of this book. Anne Young, my Editor at British Library Publications; Sally Brown, Senior Curator of Modern Literary Manuscripts, The British Library; Pete and Carol Lilleker; and, in particular, John Walker, to whom I dedicate this work.

Dominic Shellard
June 1998

Elizabethan England

The Effect of the Reformation

The sixteenth century was one of the most eventful periods in the history of England. It began with fundamental religious upheaval that would reverberate throughout the reigns of successive Tudor and Stuart monarchs, and ended in a golden age for art, science, literature and particularly drama. The career of William Shakespeare, who was born in 1564, was shaped by many of these events and it is necessary at the outset of any account of his life to be aware of the context in which he was living.

The defining event of the century was the creation of an independent Protestant Church of England and the rejection of the previously dominant Roman Catholicism and the authority of the pope. Frustrated by the lack of a male heir from his first marriage to Catherine of Aragon, Henry VIII decided, in 1527, that he wished to have the union annulled. Six years of persuasion, threat and coercion followed, as the king attempted to persuade the pope that he should be granted his wish and be permitted to marry Anne Boleyn - but it was to no avail. Rome was implacable. The only hope seemed to be the suggestion from Thomas Cromwell that Henry should end the pope's jurisdiction in England by creating himself the 'Supreme Head of the Church of England' and become the master of his own fate. The result was the Act of Supremacy in 1534, which made Henry the supreme head of the new English religion, and the subsequent dissolution of the Catholic monasteries that resulted in vandalism and desecration between 1536 and 1540.

Henry had secretly married Anne in January 1533, presumably because Anne was pregnant with the future Elizabeth I, but one should be careful not to view the break with Rome as a matter of simple expediency on the part of an impatient king. There had been a tradition of hostility to the Catholic Church in England for the previous 150 years, since the clergy were perceived by the laity as being venal, immoral and corrupt. One only has to read Chaucer's satirical portrayals of the Monk, The Summoner and The Pardoner in the *General Prologue to the Canterbury Tales* (written in 1387) to appreciate how enduring this feeling had become.

Opposite page, top:

Christopher Saxton's map of England and Wales, 1583.

British Library Maps C.7.c.1.

Opposite page, bottom left:

King Henry VIII (born 1491, crowned 1509, died 1547), painted by an unknown artist.

National Portrait Gallery

Opposite page, bottom right:

Anne Boleyn, second wife of Henry VIII (married 1533, executed 1536) and mother of Elizabeth I, painted by an unknown artist.

National Portrait Gallery

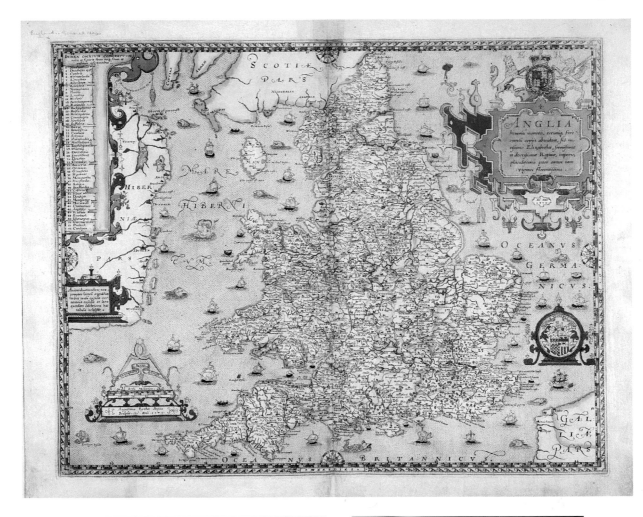

Description of The Pardoner from Chaucer's *General Prologue*

...in his male he hadde a pilwe-beer,	in his baggage; pillow-case
Which that he seyde was Oure Lady veil:	
He seyde that he hadde a gobet of the seil	fragment
That Seint Peter hadde, whan that he wente	
Upon the see, til Jhesu Crist him hente.	called him to be his disciple
He hadde a crois of latoun ful of stones,	cheap metal cross
And in a glas he hadde pigges bones.	
But with thise relikes, whan that he fond	
A povre person dwellinge upon the lond,	
Upon a day he gat him moore moneye	
Than that the person gat in monthes tweye;	he made more money in one day from these relics than the poor person did in two months

Therefore, the reforming of the practices of the Catholic Church in England - the Reformation - had its roots both in the desire of Henry VIII for an unobtainable divorce and the perceived immorality of the clergy. The ability to pray directly to God without the necessary intercession of a hierarchy of priests, bishops and cardinals was a theological reflection of this desire to simplify church practice.

For all the attempts by Henry VIII to secure a male heir - he married six wives in total - it is ironic that he was to be succeeded on his death by his sickly son from his marriage to Jane Seymour, Edward. Only nine years old when he became king, the boy-king's 'interests' were cared for by two Lord Protectors: Edward, Duke of Somerset, and then John, Duke of Northumberland. It was a period of court machinations and factionalism and although the First Protestant Prayer Book was introduced as the sole form of worship in 1549, the health of the new national religion seemed as precarious as that of the adolescent king.

English Monarchs from Henry VII to James I

Henry VII married Elizabeth of York (1485-1509)

Catherine of Aragon married Arthur (died 1502)	**Henry VIII** (1509-1547) married	Margaret Tudor (died 1541) married	Mary Tudor (died 1533)

(1) Catherine of Aragon married 1509	(2) Anne Boleyn (married 1533 executed 1536)	(3) Jane Seymour (married 1536 died 1537)	(1) James IV of Scotland (died 1513)	(2) Archibald

Mary I
(1553-1558)
married
Philip II of Spain
(died 1598)

Elizabeth I
(1558-1603)

Edward VI
(1547-1553)

James V of Scotland (died 1542)
married
(1) Madeleine (2) Mary of Guise

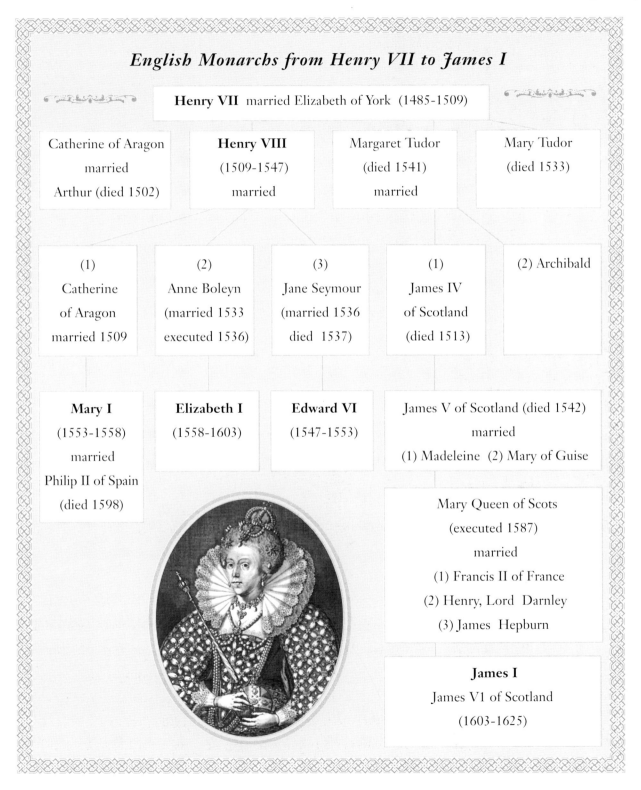

Mary Queen of Scots
(executed 1587)
married
(1) Francis II of France
(2) Henry, Lord Darnley
(3) James Hepburn

James I
James V1 of Scotland
(1603-1625)

William Shakespeare

FROM THE ORIGINAL BY S. H. GRIMM

THE PROCESSIO
FROM THE *TOWER* OF *LONDON* TO *WEST*

This was confirmed after the death of Edward VI in 1553 when his sister, Mary, acceded to the throne. Mary considered it to be her divine duty to restore Catholicism to the nation and she quickly repealed all the anti-Papal laws that had been passed since 1529, inflamed nationalistic sentiment by marrying the Catholic

12

F KING EDWARD VI.

'ER, FEB. XIX, MDXLVII, PREVIOUS TO HIS CORONATION.

Prince Philip of Spain in 1554 and presided over the burning for heresy of almost 300 Protestant martyrs between 1555 and 1558. Little wonder that she has come to be known as 'Bloody Mary', yet she, too, was to die disappointed at the prospects after her reign - for the next in line was the young Protestant princess, Elizabeth.

The procession of King Edward VI before his coronation at Westminster (1547).

Society of Antiquaries

Elizabeth's Inheritance

The legacy of the previous four decades did not bode well for Elizabeth. The country had swung from one religion to another, it had been virtually bankrupted by her father's foreign wars and there were nagging doubts about her own legitimacy. Some of her enemies would try to make something of the fact that she had been conceived before her parents had married. In this context, Shakespeare's history plays (*Richard II, Henry IV Parts 1 and 2, Henry V, Richard III, Henry VI Parts 1, 2 and 3, Henry VIII*), which with much historical revisionism collectively assert the legitimacy of the Tudor line by tracing Elizabeth's 'pure' heritage right back to the idealised King Edward I, could be read as valuable pieces of propaganda for the queen.

In addition to these historical burdens, at the time of Elizabeth's coronation England had recently suffered its worst harvests of the century (1555-57), the populace was only just recovering from a ravaging epidemic of the plague, and there were early signs of increasing inflation and unemployment brought about by a rapidly expanding population. It would be a major achievement simply to feed the nation.

Life in Elizabethan England

Population (millions)		Life Expectancy	Wages (per day)
1561	2.98		10*d* (Craftsman)/6*d* (Labourer)
1571	3.27		
1581	3.59	41.7 years	
1591	3.89	35.5 years	
1601	4.10		12*d* (Craftsman)/8*d* (Labourer)

A common view of the reign of Elizabeth I (1558-1603) is one of courtly splendour and unalloyed triumph, but this is a misconception. Foreign threat and domestic insecurity are as much a feature as military victory and artistic endeavour. In the face of Mary's legacy, the overriding aim of Elizabeth's rule in the 1560s was to achieve a measure of stability, given her precarious position. Therefore she quickly re-established Protestantism as the national religion with the Church Settlement of 1559, negotiated a peace with the ancient enemy of Scotland (the Treaty of Edinburgh, 1560) and secured a truce with another old adversary, France, in 1564 (the Treaty of Troyes). In 1562, however, a mere four years into her reign Elizabeth almost died of smallpox and this provided an early airing for three constant concerns during the next forty years: would the queen marry, would she bear an heir and who would succeed her if she died childless? The issue of procreation is one that obsesses the poet persona in the first 18 of Shakespeare's sonnets:

> *When I do count the clock that tells the time,*
> *And see the brave day sunk in hideous night;*
> *When I behold the violet past prime,*
> *And sable curls all silver'd o'er with white;*
> *When lofty trees I see barren of leaves,*
> *Which erst from heat did canopy the herd,*
> *And summer's green all girded up in sheaves*
> *Borne on the bier with white and bristly beard;*
> *Then of thy beauty do I question make*
> *That thou among the wastes of time must go,*
> *Since sweets and beauties do themselves forsake,*
> *And die as fast as they see others grow;*
> *And nothing' gainst Time's scythe can make defence*
> *Save breed, to brave him when he takes thee hence.*

(Sonnet 12, written before 1594?, published 1609)

The court was also to shudder in 1564 when the queen succumbed to 'the flux' (an early term for dysentery), and in 1572, when she was struck down by a severe fever.

Elizabeth's Achievement

Plague was not the only threat to Elizabeth's existence, however. The unwelcome arrival in England of Mary Queen of Scots in 1568 was to cause twenty years of difficulty, since Mary held pretensions to the English throne by virtue of the fact that her grandmother had been the younger sister of Henry VIII, Margaret Tudor (*see page 11*). The Reformation continued to generate hostility abroad, with Pope Pius V excommunicating Elizabeth in 1570, reflecting the view of Catholic Europe that the queen of England was a heretic, and Jesuits (the much feared members of the 'Society of Jesus' determined to spread the Catholic faith amongst 'heathens') began to arrive from 1580 from Rome with a mission to reconvert England to Catholicism. But for all the direct plots against Elizabeth's life between 1570 and 1585 (including ones by Ridolfi (1571), Throckmorton (1583) and Babington (1586)), this was predominantly a time of peace for the population at large. English men and women were less concerned with dynastic plots than a general decline in living standards as the population grew. Although 90 per cent of the Elizabethan population lived in the country, the rise in rents, the enclosure of the commons (which prevented the people from farming or grazing their cattle on previously open land) and the lack of paid employment all resulted in a drift towards the towns. Between 1560 and 1625, the population of London grew by approximately 5,600 inhabitants per year, so that by the end of Elizabeth's reign (1603), the capital numbered 215,000 citizens – half of all the people living in English towns. Shakespeare was following a growing trend when he relocated from Stratford to London in the late 1580s.

Mary's complicity in the Babington plot to murder Elizabeth resulted in her execution in 1587 and this was quickly followed in 1588 by Philip of Spain's attempt to eliminate the irritant of the heretic isle once and for all through the Spanish Armada. The repelling of this invasion force owed as much to the weather as to naval strategy, but it reinforced the growing cult of a proud, courageous and stoical queen. Pageants were held on Accession Day (17 November) creating the legend of Elizabeth as the Vestal Virgin of the Reformed Religion. Works of poetry, such as Edmund Spenser's *The Faerie Queene* and Philip Sydney's *Arcadia*, added to this atmosphere of quasi-religious reverence; Elizabethan painting reinforced the

William Shakespeare

The execution of Mary, Queen of Scots. Contemporary drawing from the papers of Robert Beale, Clerk of the Council. Beale carried the death warrant to Fotheringay and read it out before the execution. The drawing depicts Mary at three stages of the proceedings 1) entering the hall 2) attended by her women on the scaffold and 3) with her head on the block awaiting the strike of the axe.

British Library
Add. MS 48027, f.650

Extract from Spenser's *A Ditty - In Praise of Eliza, Queen of the Shepherds*

See here she sits upon the grassie greene,

(O seemly sight!)

Yclad in Scarlot, like a mayden Queene,   dressed

And ermines white:

Upon her head a Cremosin coronet

With Damaske rose and Daffadilles set:

Bay leaves betweene,

And primroses greene,

Embellish the sweete Violet.

message of the determined Virgin Queen sacrificing personal feelings for national duty. Elizabeth herself distributed portrait miniatures to particularly favoured courtiers as if they were religious icons. The contrast between appearance and reality (a favourite theme of Shakespeare's tragedies) was marked, however, since observers noted the queen's increasingly extravagant attire, low-cut dresses, unconvincing wigs and rotten teeth. She also now took to placing a perfumed silk handkerchief in her mouth whenever she greeted visitors.

  In the final decade of her reign, the themes of foreign threat, economic plight and domestic insurrection are as apparent as in the first. Uprisings in Ireland, the worst run of bad harvests the century was to witness (1594-97) and the abortive

The Spanish Armada off Portland and the Isle of Wight, 1588. One of a set of eleven maps showing each stage of the arrival and defeat of the Spanish Armada. Engraved from drawings by Robert Adams.

British Library, Maps C.7.c.1

19

SCENO·
SYSTEMATIS
PTOLE·

Elizabethan England

A map of the Ptolemaic System, with the Earth at the centre of the solar system and the crystal spheres keeping the other planets in a perfect alignment, a theory that was soon to be discredited by Copernicus.
From Andreas Cellarius, Atlas Coelestis seu Harmonica Macrocosmica, *1660.*

British Library Maps C.6.c.2

The Doubt of Future Foes A poem by Elizabeth I (c.1568)

The doubt of future foes exiles my present joy,

And wit me warns to shun such snares as threaten mine annoy.   safety

For falsehood now doth flow, and subject faith doth ebb,

Which would not be, if reason ruled or wisdom weaved the web.

But clouds of toys untried do cloak aspiring minds,

Which turn to rain of late repent, by course of changèd winds.

The top of hope supposed, the root of ruth will be,   pain

And fruitless all their graffèd guiles, as shortly ye shall see.   cunning plots

The dazzled eyes with pride, which great ambition blinds,

Shall be unsealed by worthy wights whose foresight falsehood finds.   men

The daughter of debate, that eke discord doth sow   Mary, Queen of Scots; also

Shall reap no gain where former rule hath taught still peace to grow.

No foreign banished wight shall anchor in this port,   man

Our realm it brooks no stranger's force, let them elsewhere resort.   endures

Our rusty sword with rest, shall first his edge employ

To poll their tops that seek such change and gape for joy.   Remove their heads

rebellion of her former favourite, the Earl of Essex, in 1601 all continued the depressing trends. But Elizabeth's brilliant manipulation of the rival groupings at court, the skilful handling of the question of the succession (James VI of Scotland peacefully acceded to the English throne as James I on her death on 24 March 1603) and the preservation of the nation state were success alone. That the second half of her reign had also nurtured a growing interest in foreign exploration, a widening of scientific horizons, an explosion of literary and dramatic output and the first thirty-nine years of William Shakespeare's life, meant that Elizabeth I can plausibly be said to have approached her own carefully crafted self-image.

≈ *Stratford*

Mary Arden and John Shakespeare

T he Shakespeare Birthplace Trust in Stratford-upon-Avon today maintains five buildings connected with the playwright's life: Mary Arden's House, The Birthplace in Henley Street, Anne Hathaway's Cottage, Nash's House and Hall's Croft. A visual inspection of the first two, the homes of his mother and father, suggests that Shakespeare was born into relatively comfortable circumstances.

Situated at Wilmcote, four miles west of Stratford, Mary Arden's house clearly belonged to a family of some means. Directly next door to the timber-framed property is a large stone dovecote containing 657 boxes for birds to roost. Doves were kept in the sixteenth century less for their eggs than for their meat - the young birds, the squabs, were considered a luxury food - and the close proximity of the structure, only a few feet from the main buildings, implies that the family were prepared to endure the smell and the noise of the birds to reduce the chances of an undetected theft of their prize goods. Even today, this structure is impressive and its distinctiveness is emphasised by the knowledge that its construction was dependent on obtaining a special licence from the king.

Robert Arden, Mary's father, was a substantial yeoman farmer and a very wealthy man. The family home alone, probably built around 1450 and virtually unaltered since the Ardens departed in the 1610s, testifies to this. The height of the roof (often a measure of affluence given the cost of building materials), the number of windows and the fact that three buildings have been converted into one (large enough for the parents and their eight daughters) all convey a sense of importance. In his will of 24 November 1556 Robert left goods and chattels valued at £77 11*s*. 10*d* and some historians consider this to be the bequest of a millionaire in today's currency.

Mary, who had been born around 1540, was Robert Arden's youngest daughter, but this did not prevent her from benefiting, in November 1556, from her father's will. He left her £6, 13*s*. 4*d*., the estate of Asbies which she owned outright, a cottage and nearly 60 acres with 'the crop apone the grounde sowne and tyllide hitt as it is' ('the crop upon the ground and tilled as it is'). Clearly, the seventeen-year-old Mary was something of a catch and in 1557 she married John Shakespeare, whose father, Richard, had been a husbandman (a man who tills or cultivates the soil) in Snitterfield and a tenant of Robert Arden. The date of the marriage, a year after the death of Mary's father, has intrigued those who conjecture that Robert might have disapproved of the match for some reason.

The childhood home of Mary Arden, Shakespeare's mother.

John Walker

William Shakespeare's Childhood

Although John Shakespeare had originally been a tenant farmer like his father, records show that he had enjoyed a rise in his social standing throughout the 1550s. The first mention of him confirms that he had left the country for the town when in April 1552 he was fined, along with Humphrey Reynolds and Adrian Quiney, one shilling for making a dungheap *(fecerunt sterquinarium)* in Henley Street. By 1556 John was being described as a glover (someone who makes or sells gloves from animal skins) in a suit seeking the recovery of £8, but this brush with the law (one of many in his life) appears to have been a minor inconvenience. He quickly prospered in his new environment, achieving his first civic post as an ale taster in 1556 and in the same year purchasing a property in Henley Street, and a garden and a croft (a small piece of enclosed arable land) in Greenhill Street, which were joined together to form what is known today as the Birthplace. It is likely that on his marriage to Mary the couple resided in this new dwelling and they soon began a family.

Their first daughter, Joan, was born in September 1558 (the same year that her father became one of Stratford's four constables - a profession depicted with much humour in *Measure for Measure* and *Much Ado About Nothing*), but she was to die in her infancy. A second daughter, Margaret, was born four years later, but died in 1563. Their third child and first son, William, was born in 1564 and was to prove more robust. He needed to be, for on 11 July 1564 the plague struck Stratford, claiming almost 200 victims.

As with many details of the playwright's life, the precise date of his birth is fiercely contested. Church records reveal that he was baptised on 26 April 1564 and tradition has it that his birthday must fall on 23 April - conveniently St George's Day, the patron saint of England. But if one allows that children were generally baptised three days after birth, it is possible that he was actually born on 24 April 1564.

Shakespeare's Birthplace, Henley Street, Stratford.

John Walker

What is less contentious is that by the time of William's birth, John Shakespeare had become an important Stratford dignitary. Some time before 1561 he had become a member of the town council; he was now describing himself not as a husbandman but as a glover, since he signed official documents with a pair of compasses, the emblem of the trade; and between 1561 and 1563 he served as one of the two chamberlains who oversaw the property and finances of the borough.

This rise in fortune, reflecting the increasing social mobility possible with the growth of capitalism in the Elizabethan age, continued during William's childhood. On 4 July 1565, John was elected as one of the fourteen civic aldermen of Stratford; his status was such that he was appointed a Justice of the Peace; and when William was four his father achieved his highest office, that of High Bailiff (the 'Mayor'), a post he was to hold until 1571 and which meant that he presided over council meetings. Various civic records also paint an intriguing picture of an active businessman, a respected Stratford citizen and someone not unfamiliar with the justice system. He contested a number of legal suits; he was fined for not keeping his gutters clean; he himself served on a jury; he is now referred to as 'Master' in official documents (a sign of social elevation); he became a wool-dealer; and he contributed to poor relief. As his standing grew, so did his family. Gilbert was born in 1566 (died 1612), Joan in 1569 (died 1646), Anne in 1571 (died 1579), Richard in 1574 (died 1613) and Edmund in 1580 (died 1607).

John Shakespeare's membership of the town council would have permitted him to send his children to be educated at the King's New School, Stratford, a fifteenth-century grammar school of some reputation. Unfortunately, no records exist giving details of William's education, and this has given fuel to arguments that a country lad who did not attend university could not possibly have authored the plays of the First Folio (the very first published edition of his collected works). But the lack of a document detailing the precise Stratford syllabus need not trouble us. It is likely that he attended the petty school (an Elizabethan infants school) between the age of five and seven, before entering the grammar school. Syllabi that survive from comparable institutions suggest that the instruction was broad, covering Latin and Greek literature, theology (remember how close was William's birth to the founding of the new religion) and grammar. The visits of the travelling theatre groups such as the Queen's Men (in 1569), the Earl of Worcester's Men (1569, 1576), the Countess of Essex's Men (1571), the Earl of Warwick's Men (1575) and the Earl of Leicester's Men (1573, 1576, 1579), with James Burbage at their head, also indicate that Stratford was not quite the intellectual backwater that some wish to portray. It is probable that these visiting theatre troupes performed in the ground floor gildroom (assembly room) situated beneath the first-floor classroom of the school. Perhaps the young William's dramatic imagination was initially fired by these travelling players.

The Shakespeare Family Tree

John Shakespeare = Mary Arden

died 1601   *c.*1540-1608

Joan	Margaret	**WILLIAM** = Anne Hathaway	Gilbert	Joan	Anne	Richard	Edmund
1558	1562-3	1564-1616 1556-1623	1566-1612	1569-1646	1571-1579	1574-1613	1580-1607

Susanna = John Hall   Hamnet   Judith = Thomas Quiney

1583-1649   1585-96   1585-1662

Elizabeth = 1) Thomas Nash   Shaksper   Richard   Thomas

   1608-70   died 1647   died 1617   died 1639   died 1639

            2) John Barnard

            died 1674

The death of Shakespeare's granddaughter, Elizabeth, in 1670 marked the end of his direct line.

John Shakespeare's Decline

More intriguing speculation centres on the evident - and surprising - decline in John Shakespeare's fortunes from the early 1570s. Documentary testimony is sporadic but teasing. In 1570 John was charged with making loans at an illegally high rate of interest (a fascinating fact in the light of the plot of *The Merchant of Venice*). In 1571 he was fined forty shillings for illegal wool dealing (there were strict controls on the way that wool could be sold) and in 1573 he was jointly sued by a 'whyttawer' (a dresser of hides and skins) for £30. Around 1576, when William was 12, John stopped attending the town council and after an absence of ten years, the corporation books reveal that he was replaced, in 1586, as an alderman: 'Mr Shaxpere ... doth not come to the halls when they be warned, nor hath not done of long time.'

As recently as 1569 John Shakespeare had been cited as 'Baylife, a Justice of peace, the Queenes officer & cheffe of the towne of Stratford uppon Avon' in the unsuccessful application on his behalf for a coat-of-arms, the distinctive heraldic bearings awarded to a gentleman, so how did this sudden isolation from civic affairs arise? One answer might lie in his increasing financial difficulties. In January 1578 his fellow aldermen reduced the tax that he was required to pay for the equipping of soldiers (although he still failed to maintain his contributions). In 1579 he was exempted from the weekly tax for the poor that was levied on aldermen and in the same year he sought to generate £40 by conveying (mortgaging) the Asbies property that his wife had inherited to his brother-in-law, Edmund Lambert. However, when the money was due a year later he failed to meet his debt; litigation quickly followed and in 1579, he sold a share in two houses and 100 acres that had been inherited from two of his wife's sisters for a paltry £4. But when John died in 1601 he was clearly not destitute. Granted that he was likely to have been supported in his last years by his affluent playwright son, he was still able to retain the Henley Street property, where Mary presumably lived until her death in 1607.

Perhaps financial difficulties were but a symptom of John's problems. During the 1580s there is some evidence that he was involved in potentially violent disputes. In 1580 he was fined the large sum of £40 for failing to appear in a London court to promise that he would keep the peace towards the queen and her subjects. In 1582 he petitioned for sureties of peace (injunctions that protected his safety) against four townsmen (named Ralph Cawdry, the bailiff of Stratford, William Russell, Thomas Logginge and Robert Young) 'for fear of death and mutilation of limbs'. Might this have been because John Shakespeare had professed views that would have debarred him from civic office and left him vulnerable to attack following the recommencement of religious persecution in England from 1571? The notion that William was brought up in a Catholic environment is conjecture, but one which modern scholarship is taking increasingly seriously. Documents have recently been discovered in the de Hoghton family papers in Lancashire referring to a 'William Shakeshafte', the same age as William Shakespeare, living at the house between October 1580 and July 1581 as a tutor and a 'player'. The de Hoghton family was a Catholic household. Is it conceivable that the tutor and the future playwright are one and the same person?

More concrete is John's will that was written in 1581 and is steeped in the terminology of the now suspect religion, Catholicism, with its veneration of the Virgin Mary. It begins:

> *In the name of God, the father, sonne and holy ghost, the most holy and blessed Virgin Mary, mother of God, the holy host of archangels, angels, patriarchs, prophets, evangelists, apostles, saints, martyrs and all the celestial court and company of heaven, I, John Shakspear, an unworthy member of the holy Catholick religion...calling to mind...that I may be possibly cut off in the blossome of my sins...make and ordaine this my last spiritual will...and confession of faith*

Marriage and the Lost Years

Two of the most frustrating questions for biographers of Shakespeare have been the impossibility of establishing with certainty why he relocated from Stratford to London (perhaps via Lancashire), and what happened between his marriage to Anne Hathaway in 1582 and the confirmation by Robert Greene that the playwright was active in London in 1592. What is certain is that the eighteen-year-old William married the twenty-six-year-old Anne Hathaway in November 1582. Anne was the eldest daughter of Richard Hathaway, who lived in the family home of Hewlands

Farm in Shottery, about a mile from Stratford. This property is now known as Anne Hathaway's Cottage. Anne was three months pregnant at the time of their marriage (their first child, Susanna, being baptised on 26 May 1583) and a special marriage licence was required from the Bishop of Worcester on account of her condition and Shakespeare's age – he was technically a minor. The couple's second and third children, the twins Hamnet and Judith, were born in 1585 and baptised on 2 February.

Anne Hathaway's Cottage.

John Walker

Between this date and 1592, nothing is known for certain about Shakespeare's life and they have come to be known as 'the lost years'. It was an exciting period: England came under attack from Spain and dispersed the Armada; drama proliferated in London in the late 1580s, with particularly popular works including Christopher Marlowe's *Tamburlaine* (*c*.1587) and *Dr Faustus* (*c*.1591) and Thomas Kyd's *The Spanish Tragedy* (*c*.1588); and accounts of foreign travel, such as Richard Hakluyt's *Principall Navigations, Voyages and Discoveries of the English Nation* (1589), fired the expanding collective imagination.

The first biographer of Shakespeare, Nicholas Rowe, related in the preface to his 1709 critical edition of the plays the following explanation for Shakespeare's departure from Stratford:

> *He had, by a Misfortune common enough to young Fellows, fallen into ill Company; and amongst them, some that made a frequent practice of Deer-stealing, engag'd him with them more than once in robbing a Park that belong'd to Sir Thomas Lucy of Cherlecot, near Stratford. For this he was prosecuted by that Gentleman, as he thought, somewhat too severely; and in order to revenge that ill Usage, he made a ballad upon him. And tho' this, probably the first Essay of his Poetry, be lost, yet it is said to have been so very bitter, that it redoubled the Prosecution against him to that degree, that he was oblig'd to leave his Business and Family, in Warwickshire, for some time, and shelter himself in London.*

Modern research generally discounts this story as romance, on the grounds, amongst others, that Lucy's deer reserve did not come into the family's possession until 1615.

For more certain information, we have to travel to London in 1592, where the twenty-eight year old William was already so well known in the theatre world that he was attracting spiteful comments from envious rivals.

Theatre Comes of Age

The Permanent Playhouses

The first permanent playhouse in London - The Theatre - was built in 1576 and this marked a crucial development in the evolution of English drama. Previous theatrical forms had been defined by the temporary nature of their productions. The mystery cycles (medieval religious plays), with their dramatisation of biblical episodes on large pageant wagons, had been designed for performance on religious feast days. Their spiritual heirs - morality plays such as *Mankind* - were equally mobile forms of entertainment, often performed by players in great halls or on fit-up stages erected in inn yards. The great jousts and tournaments at the court of Henry VIII were periodic pieces of theatre, whose staging was dependent on the whim of the King. These early forms already reveal the complex interweaving of drama with religion and the monarchy.

The absence of permanent playhouses did not prevent writers from producing scripts, however. The growth of printing, the increasing taste for gory visual entertainment (witness the crowds at bear-baiting and public executions), and, in particular, the influence of the Renaissance - the cultural, scientific and political rebirth of the sixteenth century - all provided encouragement for more concrete forms of theatre. Nicholas Udall's *Ralph Roister Doister* is generally considered to be the first English Renaissance comedy and it bears testimony to this new atmosphere of learning with its debt to the Roman dramatists Terence and Plautus. The play also demonstrates the appeal of writing for a particular 'company' of players with whom the playwright is familiar. In Udall's case, this was probably the boys of Eton College, where he was the headmaster. Shakespeare's career, too, would flourish once he connected himself to a familiar group of performers.

'Academic' drama was to play an increasingly important role in the development of Elizabethan theatre. The choirboys of the Chapel Royal and St Paul's Cathedral not only provided a ready-made company to workshop scripts, but served as a pool for some of the necessary female roles (women did not tread the English stage until 1660). Universities started to get in on the act as well. The first

English Renaissance tragedy, *Gorboduc*, was written by two students of the London law courts, the Inner Temple, Thomas Norton and Thomas Sackville, and performed to fellow students in 1562. Later, the possession or lack of a university education would become a source of fractious debate amongst the playwrights themselves.

The Nativity Car on a medieval pageant wagon.

Victoria and Albert Museum

By the 1570s, then, there was a market for drama staged in permanent outdoor playhouses and the carpenter, James Burbage, was the first to spot this. In 1572, the 'Acte for the punishment of Vacabondes' had, in effect, prepared the ground for the creation of permanent companies with its requirement that each company should be authorised by one nobleman or two Justices of the Peace. This patronage ensured a degree of stability and protection and meant that there was money to be made through drama - a highly appealing prospect at this time of embryonic capitalism. Burbage consequently erected The Theatre in the district of Shoreditch, to the north of the City of London and well outside its walls.

The location of this building in 1576 is significant and illustrates the differing views of the authorities to playgoing. Although the appetite for drama was large, there were continual threats to its survival. The revival of religious persecutions in the 1570s had meant the suppression of the mystery cycles for being perceived as too Catholic, given their emphasis on visual iconography, the retelling of saints' lives and the link to ritual. This trend was complemented by the increasing hostility of the Puritans (extreme protestants), who objected to theatre *per se* on the grounds that the process of mimesis - the act of taking on another role - was heretical, because actors were denying their God-given role. The Puritans controlled the City of London, hence the need for Burbage to base his theatre outside the city walls and away from their jurisdiction. The Puritans' irritation at this new venue was increased by the fact that it was apparent in the very first year of its existence that The Theatre was likely to succeed as a commercial exercise, William Harrison sourly observing that 'It is an evident token of a wicked time when plaiers waxe so riche that they can build such houses'.

The attitude of the aristocracy to this new form of entertainment was more ambivalent. Queen Elizabeth herself was a consummate actress and a skilled rhetorician. She made repeated public progresses throughout her kingdom to display herself to her subjects. She toyed with the affections of a succession of suitors to ensure the stability of her realm and she is famous for her speech to her troops on the docks at Tilbury, where she sought to stiffen their morale in the face of the Armada (no matter that they were standing on the wrong bank of the Thames to repulse an invading force!):

Richard Tarlton dressed as a clown.

Pepys' Library, Magdalene College, Cambridge

I am come amongst you,

As you see at this time,

Not for my recreation and disport,

But being resolved, in the midst and heat of the battle,

To live and die amongst you all;

To lay down for my God,

And for my kingdom,

And for my people,

My honour and my blood

Even in the dust.

I know I have the body of a weak and feeble woman,

But I have the heart and stomach of a King,

And of a King of England too!

And think foul scorn that Parma or Spain,

Or any prince of Europe,

Should dare to invade the borders of my realm!

Leading members of the court also gave their blessing to individual companies (supporting, for example, the Earl of Leicester's Men, the Lord Chamberlain's Men and the Admiral's Men) and the queen herself often enjoyed the royal command performances (there were six in the winter of 1596/7, for example, all given by the Lord Chamberlain's Men). But the gathering together of large numbers of people also posed problems of public order and possible threats of sedition. Thus, from 1581 the Master of the Revels, Edmund Tilney, was empowered with the censoring of plays and the licensing of venues. Yet again, we can see the paradoxical relationship between the court and drama - something that characterises the history of English drama right up to the abolition of stage censorship in 1968. The Master of the Revels was accountable to the Lord Chamberlain, who was responsible for organising court entertainments. Trusted companies, therefore, obtained prestigious and profitable commissions to perform in front of the royal household. But it was equally important that the companies did not overstep the mark and problematic scenes had to be suppressed. It is significant, therefore, that early single-volume editions ('quartos') of Shakespeare's *Richard II* do not contain the deposition scene, where Richard is replaced as the monarch by Henry Bolingbroke, the subsequent Henry IV. Given the uncertainty surrounding Elizabeth's succession in the 1590s, this was deemed to be too controversial, especially given Elizabeth's belief that there were uncomfortable parallels between herself and the sorry king. Its excision was almost certainly ordered by the censor.

However, the greatest threats to the new entrepreneurs, the playwrights, were those that affected their economic prospects. These included the virulence of the plague, which closed the playhouses when deaths exceeded fifty per week (in 1577, 1578, 1581, 1593 and 1603, with smaller outbreaks reducing performances in 1580,

Map of the City of London and London Playhouses ('Civitates Orbis Terrarum', 1572).
1) The Theatre;
2) The Globe;
3) The Swan.

British Library C.3603

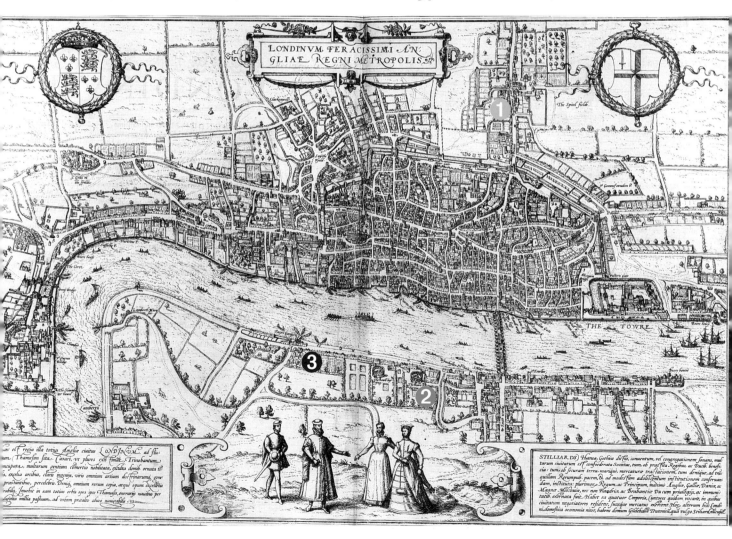

The Spanish Tragedie:
OR,
Hieronimo is mad againe.

Containing the lamentable end of *Don Horatio*, and *Belimperia*; with the pittifull death of *Hieronimo*.

Newly corrected, amended, and enlarged with new Additions of the *Painters* part, and others, as it hath of late been diuers times acted.

LONDON,
Printed by W. White, for I. White and T. Langley, and are to be sold at their Shop ouer against the Sarazens head without New-gate. 1615.

1583, 1586, 1587, 1594, 1604 and 1605); the taste of the public (if a play met with disfavour it rarely survived ten performances); and the approval of the playhouse owners, who commissioned their works. No wonder that the financially astute Shakespeare became one of the six shareholders of the Lord Chamberlain's Men to minimise his personal risk.

The construction of The Theatre was followed by the appearance of the Curtain (1577), the Rose (1587), the Swan (1595), the Globe (1599), the Fortune (1600) and the Hope (1614). This proliferation of new venues reflected the prolific output of new dramatists. Over 1,500 plays are known to have been written between 1590 and 1642, with many more likely to have remained unrecorded.

Early Elizabethan Drama

The first great work of Elizabethan drama was Thomas Kyd's *The Spanish Tragedy* (*c*.1588). Centring on the revenge of Hieronimo for his murdered son, Horatio, its mixture of intrigue in the court of an enemy country, gruesome on-stage violence (Hieronimo bites out his tongue rather than reveal his motives) and melodramatic speeches was hugely popular, and it has come to be seen as the father of a recurrent genre, the Revenge Tragedy. In its incorporation of a play within a play and its depiction of Hieronimo hovering between sanity and madness, it has also been seen as a possible source for *Hamlet*.

Kyd's friend Christopher Marlowe (1564-1593) was the first great playwright of the age. His earliest work, testifying to the vogue for collaboration, was *Dido, Queen of Carthage* with Thomas Nashe (*c*.1587) and this was quickly followed by *Tamburlaine Part 1*, and its successor, created by public demand,

Printed at London for *Iohn Wright*, and are to be fold at his fhop without Newgate, 1624.

Title-page of Christopher Marlowe's Dr Faustus.

British Library C.34.d.27

Part 2. Both works were performed by the Admiral's Men with the supreme Elizabethan actor, Edward Alleyn, in the title role. Marlowe revels in anti-heroes - Dr Faustus, for example, literally sells his soul to the devil - and it is his plays, above all, that reveal the split-personality of the late Elizabethan period. He reflects the contemporary delight in accounts of foreign countries and their mode of governance (*Tamburlaine* and *The Jew of Malta*). He appeals to the intellectual curiosity unleashed by the Renaissance (*Dr Faustus*) and the fascination of the English with their own history (*Edward II*). But it is his unorthodox views that make him such an intriguing playwright and an emblem of the age's uncertainty.

Above:

Edward Alleyn, actor (1566-1626), painted by an unknown artist.

Dulwich Picture Gallery

Above right:

Portrait thought to be of Christopher Marlowe, playwright (1564-1593).

Corpus Christi College, Cambridge

Tamburlaine is an amoral conqueror, Barabas (in *The Jew of Malta*) a remorseless serial killer, Dr Faustus a self-confessed non-believer and Edward II a celebrated homosexual.

The turbulence of Marlowe's themes is reflected in the turbulence of his life. The son of a Canterbury shoemaker, he was educated at Cambridge and was as renowned for his atheism and his outspoken opinions as he was for his drama and his intellect. He was killed in a tavern brawl in 1593, possibly because of his activities as a spy, and had overlapped with Shakespeare's stay in the capital for about three years. Partly by appropriating Marlowe's bequest to English drama - the unrhymed iambic pentameter known as blank verse ('Was this the face that launched a thousand ships?' *Dr Faustus*) - Shakespeare moved swiftly to fill the vacuum.

≈ *London to 1594*

The Upstart Crow

S hakespeare's 'lost years' between his marriage to Anne Hathaway and his first appearance in London end with a pamphlet written by an embittered and dying rival playwright. Robert Greene's *Groats-worth of Wit* (1592) contains the first reference in print to him, when in a section addressed to three of his 'fellow scholars about this city' (generally felt to be Marlowe, Nashe and Peele) he attacks Shakespeare as both a player and a writer:

> *Base-minded men all three of you, if by my mysery you be not warned; for unto none of you (like me) sought those burrs to cleave, those puppets (I mean) that spake from our mouths, those anticks garnished in our colours. Is it not strange that I, to whom they all have been beholding: is it not like that you, to whom they all have been beholding, shall (were ye in that case as I am now) be both at once of them forsaken? Yes, trust them not: for there is an upstart crow, beautified with our feathers, that with his **Tiger's heart wrapt in a player's hide**, supposes he is as well able to bombast out a blank verse as the best of you; and being an absolute **Johannes Factotum**, is in his own conceit the only Shake-scene in a country.*

From this outburst, we can deduce many things about Shakespeare's early dramatic career. He had arrived in London by the date of publication, 1592 (when he would have been twenty-eight), and had probably been active in the capital for several years before that. (Recent research conjectures that he might have joined the Queen's Men shortly after they visited Stratford in 1587.) The reference to a line from *Henry VI Part 3* ('O tiger's heart wrapt in a woman's hide' I iv 137) not only proves that this particular history play had been staged by this time, but that Shakespeare was known as both a performer in the new playhouses (Greene changes 'tyger' to 'player'), as well as a writer producing scripts for them. A tradition that flourished in the eighteenth century (as do so many of the anecdotes that help to 'fill in' the gaps about

Detail from Hollar's Long View of London showing the River Thames at Southwark.

Guildhall Library

Shakespeare's early life) claims that his first contact with the London playhouses was as a holder of horses, and Dr Samuel Johnson's 1765 edition of the plays contains the following intriguing - but unverifiable - story:

> In the time of Elizabeth, coaches being yet uncommon, and hired coaches not at all in use, those who were too proud, too tender, or too idle to walk, went on horseback to any distant business or diversion. Many came on horseback to the play, and when Shakespear fled to London from the terrour of a criminal prosecution, his first expedient was to wait at the door of the play-house, and hold the horses of those that had no servants, that they might be ready again after the performance. In this office he became so conspicuous for his care and

readiness, that in a short time every man as he alighted called for Will. Shakespear, and scarcely any other waiter was trusted with a horse while Will. Shakespear could be had. This was the first dawn of better fortune. Shakespear finding more horses put into his hand than he could hold, hired boys to wait under his inspection, who, when Will. Shakespear was summoned, were immediately to present themselves, I am Shakespear's boy, Sir. In time Shakespear found higher employment, but as long as the practice of riding to the play-house continued, the waiters that held the horses retained the appellation of Shakespear's Boys.

Note how the 'deer-poaching' myth (first mentioned by Rowe in 1709) has already gained currency as accepted fact by the mid-eighteenth century, a not uncommon feature of Shakespeare biography throughout the ages. What is less hypothetical is that by 1592 Shakespeare's plays were already attracting significant attention - Greene scathingly refers to him as a self-styled universal genius ('Johannes Factotum') - and the famous reference to him as 'an upstart crow' suggests that he was viewed as a commercial, as well as an intellectual, rival. This is a vital point. In the late Elizabethan age playwrights were writing as much for money as for Art and competition was intense, particularly given the demand for new works and the short period between commission and production. Greene's charge that Shakespeare has been 'beautified with our feathers' reflects this cut-throat environment. Against this catalogue of accusations, Greene's assertion that Shakespeare is 'as well able to bombast out blank verse as the best of you' could be taken as a stunning compliment!

The First Dawn of Better Fortune

The swift rebuttal of Greene's charges by Thomas Nashe, who denounced the book as 'a scald, trivial, lying pamphlet' reveals that not everybody held such a low opinion of the Stratford playwright, and the profuse apology to both Marlowe and Shakespeare for the work three months after Greene's death by his editor, Henry Chettle, also gives a further insight into Shakespeare's standing at this early part of his career:

I am as sorry as if the original fault had been my fault, because myself have seen his demeanour no less civil than he excellent in the quality [i.e. acting] he professes. Besides, divers of worship have reported his uprightness of dealing, which argues his honesty, and his facetious grace in writing, that approves his art.

(Preface to Kind-Heart's Dream, *December 1592)*

How had Shakespeare come to such public notice so quickly? Dating his plays is a notoriously difficult process, but it is likely that by 1592 he was already the author of the tragedies, *Titus Andronicus* and *Romeo and Juliet*, the comedies *The Two Gentlemen of Verona, The Taming of the Shrew, Love's Labour's Lost* and *A Midsummer Night's Dream* and the history plays, *Henry VI (Parts 1, 2 and 3), Richard III* and *King John*.

Early Tragedies

These early works all share features that were to crop up again and again in Shakespeare's plays: his use of a wide range of sources, his eye for a good story, his readiness to adapt the source material to his own dramatic ends, the influence of the era in which he was writing and his abiding sense of the theatrical. *Titus Andronicus* (performed by Strange's Men on 6 January 1593) is possibly the earliest tragedy and demonstrates immediately Shakespeare's engagement with contemporary England. Although set in ancient Rome, it is a play about a burning Elizabethan issue - that of the right of succession, given that the queen had no children - and it begins with the grizzled Roman general, Titus Andronicus, forced to arbitrate between the rival claims to the title of Emperor by the brothers Saturninus and Bassianus. Titus's choice of the former and his refusal to grant mercy to the son of Saturninus's eventual wife, Tamora, proves to be a crucial mistake and a catalogue of gruesome events then follows. These reflect the Elizabethans' love of public executions and bear-baiting as much as the literary taste for the gory works of Seneca and the genre of Revenge Tragedy. As the play progresses, Titus's daughter, Lavinia, is raped, before having her hands cut off and her tongue ripped out to prevent identification of her attackers; Titus is also tricked into cutting his own hand off in the mistaken

Opposite page:

A scene from
Titus Andronicus
- the only extant contemporary drawing of Elizabethan performers. Note the mixture of Elizabethan and Roman costume.

The Library, Longleat House

Written by Henry Peacham – author of the
Compleat gentleman

Tamora
pleading

Enter Tamora pleadinge for her sonnes
goiny to execution

Tam: Stay Romane bretheren gratious Conquerors
Victorious Titus rewe the teares I shed
A mothers teares in passion off her sonnes
And iff thy sonnes weare ever deare to thee
Oh, thinke my sonnes to bee as deare to mee
Suffizeth not that wee are brought to Roome
To beautifye thy triumphes and returne
Captive to thee and to thy Romane yoake
But must my sonnes be slaughtered in the streetes
for valiant Doynges in their Cuntryes cause
Oh iff to fight for kinge and Common weale
Weere pietye in thine it is in these
Andronicus staine not thy tombe wo blood
Will thou drawe neere the nature off the Gods
Drawe neere them then in beinge mercifull
Sweete mercy is nobilityes true badge
Thryce noble Titus spare my first borne sonne

Titus   Patient your selfe madame for dy hee must
        Aaron do you likewise prepare your selfe

Aron: And now at last repent your missed liffe
        Oh: now I curse the day and yet I thinke
        few comes withim the compass off my curse
        wherein I did not some notorious ill
        As kill a man or els devise his death
        Ravish a mayd or plott the way to do it
        Accuse some innocent and forsweare my selfe
        Set deadly enmity betweene to freendes
        Make poore mens cattell breake theire neckes
        Set fire on barnes and haystackes in the night
        And bid the owners quentch them wo their teares
        Oft have I digd vp dead men from their graues
        And set them vprights at their deere freendes dore
        Even almost when theire sorrowes was forgott
        And on their Bresses as on the barke off trees
        Haue with my knife carved in Romane letters
        Lett not your sorrowe dy thoughti I am dead
        Tut I have done a thousand dreadfull thinges
        As willingly as one would kill a fly
        And nothing greiues mee hartily indeede
        for that I cannot do ten thousand more   &c:

So far
from
Shakspeer
Titus
andronicus
Sc. 2

Henricus Peacham
Anno m° q° q° q°

Harbm

Extract from Titus Andronicus in the First Folio showing the multiple deaths at the end of the play (V iii 34–66).

British Library C.39.k.15

The Tragedie of Titus Andronicus. 51

Hath ordained to an Honourable end,
For Peace, for Loue, for League, and good to Rome :
Please you therfore draw nie and take your places.
  Satur. Marcus we will.   *Hoboyes.*
          A Table brought in.
  *Enter Titus like a Cooke, placing the meat on
  the Table, and Lauinia with a vale ouer her face.*

  Titus. Welcome my gracious Lord,
Welcome Dread Queene,
Welcome ye Warlike Gothes, welcome *Lucius,*
And welcome all : although the cheere be poore,
T'will fill your stomacks, please you eat of it.
  Sat. Why art thou thus attir'd *Andronicus* ?
  Ti. Because I would be sure to haue all well,
To entertaine your Highnesse, and your Empresse.
  Tam. We are beholding to you good *Andronicus* ?
  Tit. And if your Highnesse knew my heart, you were:
My Lord the Emperour resolue me this,
Was it well done of rath *Virginius,*
To slay his daughter with his owne right hand,
Because she was enfor'st, stain'd, and deflowr'd ?
  Satur. It was *Andronicus.*
  Tit. Your reason, Mighty Lord ?
  Sat. Because the Girle, should not suruiue her shame,
And by her presence still renew his sorrowes.
  Tit. A reason mighty, strong, and effectuall,
A patterne, president, and liuely warrant,
For me (most wretched) to performe the like:
Die, die, *Lauinia,* and thy shame with thee,
And with thy shame, thy Fathers sorrow die.
                              He kils her.
  Sat. What hast done, vnnaturall and vnkinde ?
  Tit. Kil'd her for whom my teares haue made me blind,
I am as wofull as *Virginius* was,
And haue a thousand times more cause then he.
  Sat. What was she rauisht ? tell who did the deed,
  Tit. Wilt please you eat,
Wilt please your Hignesse feed ?
  Tam. Why hast thou slaine thine onely Daughter ?
  Titus. Not I, 'twas *Chiron* and *Demetrius,*
They rauisht her, and cut away her tongue,
And they, 'twas they, that did her all this wrong.
  Satu. Go fetch them hither to vs presently.
  Tit. Why there they are both, baked in that Pie,
Whereof their Mother daintily hath fed,
Eating the flesh that she herselfe hath bred.
'Tis true, 'tis true, witnesse my kniues sharpe point.
                          He stabs the Empresse.
  Satu. Die frantick wretch, for this accursed deed,
  Luc. Can the Sonnes eye, behold his Father bleed ?
There's meede for meede, death for a deadly deed.
  Mar. You sad fac'd men, people and Sonnes of Rome,
By vprores seuer'd like a flight of Fowle,
Scattred by windes and high tempestuous gusts :
Oh let me teach you how, to knit againe
This scattred Corne, into one mutuall sheafe,
These broken limbs againe into one body.
  Goth. Let Rome herselfe be bane vnto herselfe,
And shee whom mightie kingdomes cursie too,
Like a forlorne and desperate castaway,
Doe shamefull execution on her selfe.
But if my frostie signes and chaps of age,
Graue witnesses of true experience,
Cannot induce you to attend my words,
Speake Romes deere friend, as 'erst our Aunceftor,

When with his solemne tongue he did discourse
To loue-sicke *Didoes* sad attending eare,
The story of that balefull burning night,
When subtill Greekes surpriz'd King *Priams* Troy:
Tell vs what *Sinon* hath bewicht our eares,
Or who hath brought the fatall engine in,
That giues our Troy, our Rome the ciuill wound.
My heart is not compact of flint nor steele,
Nor can I vtter all our bitter griefe,
But floods of teares will drowne my Oratorie,
And breake my very vtterance, euen in the time
When it should moue you to attend me most,
Lending your kind hand Commiseration.
Heere is a Captaine, let himtell the tale,
Your hearts will throb and weepe to heare him speake,
  Luc. This Noble Auditory, be it knowne to you,
That cursed *Chiron* and *Demetrius,*
Were they that murdred our Emperours Brother,
And they it were that rauished our Sister,
For their fell faults our Brothers were beheaded,
Our Fathers teares despis'd, and basely cousen'd,
Of that true hand that fought Romes quarrell out,
And sent her enemies vnto the graue,
Lastly, my selfe vnkindly banished,
The gates shut on me, and turn'd weeping out,
To beg reliefe among Romes Enemies,
Who drown'd their enmity in my true teares,
And op'd their armes to imbrace me as a Friend :
And I am turned forth, be it knowne to you,
That haue preferu'd her welfare in my blood,
And from her bosome tooke the Enemies point,
Sheathing the steele in my aduentrous body.
Alas you know, I am no Vaunter I,
My scars can witnesse, dumbe although they are,
That my report is iust and full of truth:
But soft, me thinkes I do digresse too much,
Cyting my worthlesse praise: Oh pardon me,
For when no Friends are by, men praise themselues,
  Marc. Now is my turne to speake. Behold this Child,
Of this was *Tamora* deliuered,
The issue of an Irreligious *Moore,*
Chiefe Architect and plotter of these woes,
The Villaine is aliue in *Titus* house,
And as he is, to witnesse this is true.
Now iudge what course had *Titus* to reuenge
These wrongs, vnspeakeable past patience,
Or more then any liuing man could beare.
Now you haue heard the truth, what say you Romaines ?
Haue we done ought amisse ? shew vs wherein,
And from the place where you behold vs now,
The poore remainder of *Andronici,*
Will hand in hand all headlong cast vs downe,
And on the ragged stones beat forth our braines,
And make a mutuall closure of our house :
Speake Romaines speake, and if you say we shall,
Loe hand in hand, *Lucius* and I will fall.
  Emili. Come come, thou reuerent man of Rome,
And bring our Emperour gently in thy hand,
Lucius our Emperour : for well I know,
The common voyce do cry it shall be so.
  Mar. Lucius, all haile Romes Royall Emperour,
Goe, goe into old *Titus* sorrowfull house,
And hither hale that misbelieuing *Moore,*
To be adiudg'd some direfull slaughtering death,
As punishment for his most wicked life.
Lucius all haile to Romes gracious Gouernour.
                              Lucius
                    ee 2

belief that this will save his sons, Martius and Quintus, from execution; and the action climaxes with a feast organised by Titus in which he serves the heads of Demetrius and Chiron baked in a pie to their wicked mother, Tamora, before the infamous four murders in

20 lines that conclude the circle of revenge. Lest one think that Shakespeare must have had a warped imagination to invent all of this, his source for Lavinia's mutilation had impeccable literary credentials - the myth of Philomel to be found in Ovid's *Metamorphoses*. Stark, compelling and not as unsophisticated as is sometimes claimed, the moral of *Titus Andronicus* is clear: one false step in the question of succession and the consequences for the realm will be dire.

Titus Andronicus is also the only work for which we have a contemporary Elizabethan drawing showing what the tragedians may have been wearing *(see page 45)*. In the Peacham drawing (dated 1595 or 1599), Tamora and two of her three sons are seen kneeling before Titus and begging for the life of her eldest son, Alarbus. To the far right stands the amoral Moor, Aaron, and to the far left two soldiers. Their costumes are an intriguing mixture of Elizabethan and Roman dress. Titus is holding a spear and wearing a toga and a garland of leaves, whereas the soldiers are clad in Elizabethan clothing. Whether the drawing is an imaginative recreation or a faithful record is still the subject of debate.

Romeo and Juliet falls more readily into the category of timeless tragedy. The story of the two 'star-cross'd lovers' caught between the warring factions of the Capulets and the Montagues has often been seen as a metaphor for all the innocent victims of senseless conflicts. It is also much-loved for its depiction of adolescent romance, its powerful sense of inexorable fate and its plethora of memorable phrases. The balcony scene in Act II ii, where Romeo gazes up in awe at the radiant Juliet, is one of the most famous stage images in world drama –

> *But soft! what light through yonder window breaks?*
> *It is the east, and Juliet is the sun!*
> *Arise, fair sun, and kill the envious moon,*
> *Who is already sick and pale with grief*
> *That thou her maid art far more fair than she. (II ii 2-5)*

- and Juliet's unprompted response

> *O Romeo, Romeo! wherefore art thou Romeo? (II ii 33)*

one of the most famous lines.

Mer. *Romeo*, Humours, Madman, Passion, Louer,
Appeare thou in the likenesse of a sigh,
Speake but one rime, and I am satisfied:
Cry me but ay me, Prouant, but Loue and day,
Speake to my goship *Venus* one faire word,
One Nickname for her purblind Sonne and her,
Young *Abraham Cupid* he that shot so true,
When King *Cophetua* lou'd the begger Maid,
He heareth not, he stirreth not, he moueth not,
The Ape is dead, I must coniure him,
I coniure thee by *Rosalines* bright eyes,
By her High forehead, and her Scarlet lip,
By her Fine foote, Straight leg, and Quiuering thigh,
And the Demeanes, that there Adiacent lie,
That in thy likenesse thou appeare to vs.

Ben. And if he heare thee thou wilt anger him.

Mer. This cannot anger him, t'would anger him
To raise a spirit in his Mistresse circle,
Of some strange nature, letting it stand
Till she had laid it, and coniured it downe,
That were some spight.
My inuocation is faire and honest, & in his Mistris name,
I coniure onely but to raise vp him.

Ben. Come, he hath hid himselfe among these Trees
To be consorted with the Humerous night:
Blind is his Loue, and best befits the darke.

Mer. If Loue be blind, Loue cannot hit the marke,
Now will he sit vnder a Medler tree,
And wish his Mistresse were that kind of Fruite,
As Maides call Medlers when they laugh alone,
O *Romeo* that she were, O that she were
An open, or thou a Poprin Peare,
Romeo goodnight, Ile to my Truckle bed,
This Field-bed is to cold for me to sleepe,
Come shall we go?

Ben. Go then, for 'tis in vaine to seeke him here
That meanes not to be found.   *Exeunt.*

Rom. He ieasts at Scarres that neuer felt a wound,
But soft, what light through yonder window breaks?
It is the East, and *Iuliet* is the Sunne,
Arise faire Sun and kill the enuious Moone,
Who is already sicke and pale with griefe,
That thou her Maid art far more faire then she:
Be not her Maid since she is enuious,
Her Vestal liuery is but sicke and greene,
And none but fooles do weare it, cast it off:
It is my Lady, O it is my Loue, O that she knew she were,
She speakes, yet she sayes nothing, what of that?
Her eye discourses, I will answere it:
I am too bold 'tis not to me she speakes:
Two of the fairest starres in all the Heauen,
Hauing some businesse do entreat her eyes,
To twinckle in their Spheres till they returne.
What if her eyes were there, they in her head,
The brightnesse of her cheeke would shame those starres,
As day-light doth a Lampe, her eye in heauen,
Would through the ayrie Region streame so bright,
That Birds would sing, and thinke it were not night:
See how she leanes her cheeke vpon her hand.
O that I were a Gloue vpon that hand,
That I might touch that cheeke.

Iul. Ay me.

Rom. She speakes.
Oh speake againe bright Angell, for thou art
As glorious to this night being ore my head,
As is a winged messenger of heauen

Vnto the white vpturned wondring eyes
Of mortalls that fall backe to gaze on him,
When he bestrides the lazie puffing Cloudes,
And sailes vpon the bosome of the ayre.

Iul. O *Romeo, Romeo*, wherefore art thou *Romeo* ?
Denie thy Father and refuse thy name:
Or if thou wilt not, be but sworne my Loue,
And Ile no longer be a *Capulet.*

Rom. Shall I heare more, or shall I speake at this?

Iu. 'Tis but thy name that is my Enemy:
Thou art thy selfe, though not a *Mountague*,
What's *Mountague* ? it is nor hand nor foote,
Nor arme, nor face, O be some other name
Belonging to a man.
What? in a names that which we call a Rose,
By any other word would smell as sweete,
So *Romeo* would, were he not *Romeo* cal'd,
Retaine that deare perfection which he owes,
Without that title *Romeo*, doffe thy name,
And for thy name which is no part of thee,
Take all my selfe.

Rom. I take thee at thy word:
Call me but Loue, and Ile be new baptiz'd,
Hence foorth I neuer will be *Romeo.*

Iuls. What man art thou, that thus bescreen'd in night
So stumblest on my counsell?

Rom. By a name,
I know not how to tell thee who I am:
My name deare Saint, is hatefull to my selfe,
Because it is an Enemy to thee,
Had I it written, I would teare the word.

Iuli. My eares haue yet not drunke a hundred words
Of thy tongues vttering, yet I know the sound.
Art thou not *Romeo*, and a *Montague*?

Rom. Neither faire Maid, if either thee dislike.

Iul. How cam'st thou hither,
Tell me, and wherefore?
The Orchard walls are high, and hard to climbe,
And the place death, considering who thou art,
If any of my kinsmen find thee here.

Rom. With Loues light wings
Did I ore-perch these Walls,
For stony limits cannot hold Loue out,
And what Loue can do, that dares Loue attempt:
Therefore thy kinsmen are no stop to me.

Iul. If they do see thee, they will murther thee.

Rom. Alacke there lies more perill in thine eye,
Then twenty of their Swords, looke thou but sweete,
And I am proofe against their enmity.

Iul. I would not for the world they saw thee here.

Rom. I haue nights cloake to hide me from their eyes
And but thou loue me, let them finde me here,
My life were better ended by their hate,
Then death proroged wanting of thy Loue.

Iul. By whose direction found'st thou out this place?

Rom. By Loue that first did promp me to enquire,
He lent me counsell, and I lent him eyes,
I am no Pylot, yet wert thou as far
As that vast-shore-washet with the farthest Sea,
I should aduenture for such Marchandise.

Iul. Thou knowest the maske of night is on my face,
Else would a Maiden blush bepaint my cheeke,
For that which thou hast heard me speake to night,
Faine would I dwell on forme, faine, faine, denie
What I haue spoke, but farewell Complement,
Doest thou Loue ? I know thou wilt say I,

And/

Early Histories and Comedies up to the Plague (1593)

An important point to stress about Shakespeare is his versatility. Tragedies, histories, comedies - they were all forms to be mastered. The works that chronicle the reigns of Henry VI and of Richard III, written between 1590 and 1593, may not have been conceived as a group but they are all bound together by an over-arching narrative thread. Drawing on the historical accounts of Edward Hall and Raphael Holinshed, *Henry VI Parts 1, 2* and *3* and *Richard III* would have served as instruction about the dawn of the Tudor dynasty, as well as being a useful piece of propaganda for the current Tudor regime. That there was an appetite for this theatrical history lesson is evident from the success of *Henry VI Part 1*. The box office takings from its first performance by the Admiral's Men at the Rose on 3 March 1592 were £3 16*s*. 8*d*., the highest of the season according to the papers of the theatre producer Philip Henslowe (known as the *Henslowe Diaries*), and the play received another fifteen performances over the next ten months.

Richard III, Shakespeare's longest work thus far, was the first to demonstrate his ability to create a 'star role'. The hunch-backed usurper, who is so convincing that he can seduce Lady Anne over the body of her dead husband ('Was ever woman in this humour woo'd?' *Richard III*, I ii 227), has proved continually compelling, even if the naked piece of Tudor propaganda uttered by the new King Henry VII at the end of the play -

> *O, now let Richmond and Elizabeth,*
> *The true succeeders of each royal house,*
> *By God's fair ordinance conjoin together!*
> *And let their heirs - God, if thy will be so -*
> *Enrich the time to come with smooth-faced peace,*
> *With smiling plenty, and fair prosperous days!*
>
> (V v 29-34)

- now passes us by. Whether or not Shakespeare had been brought up in a Catholic household, the histories exemplify several impeccable Elizabethan creeds: the responsibility of the king to foster national unity, the suffering caused by civil discord and the need to find a balance between national welfare and self-interest, to name but three.

The popularity of individual plays has ebbed and flowed during the four centuries following Shakespeare's death. *King John*, for example, a work from this period that queries the validity of war, has rarely been performed in the twentieth century, whereas the less interesting *The Two Gentleman of Verona*, probably the earliest comedy, continues to be revived on a regular basis. However, before the watershed of 1594, three more enduring comedies were to be written: *Love's Labour's Lost*, *The Taming of the Shrew* and *A Midsummer Night's Dream*.

All of these works remind us that Shakespeare wrote his works for performance first and foremost. A reading of *Love's Labour's Lost*, which revolves around the oath that the King of Navarre and three of his lords have sworn to keep from the sight of woman, seems much dryer than an actual performance, where the complex linguistic allusions dissolve in the comedy of their attempted wooing of the princess of France and her ladies. *The Taming of the Shrew* is similarly richer when viewed by an audience. Only then can we fully appreciate that the play we are observing is actually a mocking play-within-a-play, staged by a lord for the drunken Christopher Sly. The second play deals with the taming (some would say humiliation) of Katherina by Petruchio, and Katherina's conversion from independent and feisty spirit to docile and compliant wife. Her eventual claim that

> *Thy husband is thy lord, thy life, thy keeper*
> *Thy head, thy sovereign*

provokes fierce argument today as to whether she is speaking with irony or not.

But the most visual of all Shakespeare's works is surely *A Midsummer Night's Dream*. Although Elizabethan playwrights wrote for essentially bare stages and the use of props was minimal, the appeal of the *Dream* to our imagination is immense. The escape to the wood by Hermia, Lysander, Demetrius and Helena to choose their own partners free of parental edict; the humorous quarrel between the King and Queen of the fairies, Oberon and Titania, over the changeling boy; the magical capabilities and the mischievous behaviour of the sprite, Puck; and the hilarious interaction of the Athenian tradesmen, including the comical Bottom, all combine to create one of Shakespeare's best-loved comedies. The play contains further reflection on the business of the theatre, with the tradesmen's rehearsal and performance of the ludicrous *Pyramus and Thisbe*. The scene where the lovers attempt to communicate through a wall (depicted by the stretching out of the eponymous characters' fingers) never fails to bring the house down, and, although we may agree with Hippolyta that 'This is the silliest stuff that ever I heard' it is also one of the finest sections of comedy ever written. This scene and Puck's placing of an ass's head onto Bottom goes some way to countering the notion that Shakespeare's comedies are simply not funny.

The Plague: Shakespeare Turns To Poetry

There were many practical difficulties facing playwrights in the early 1590s, not least the need to attract commissions, but by far the biggest one was the threat of plague. As early as 1569, plague regulations decreed that places of public assembly should be closed during periods of infection, and, following an epidemic in 1580, new edicts were put in place to cater for the new phenomena of public playhouses. Performances were permitted to recommence only when the weekly total of plague victims had numbered less than fifty for a three-week period (reduced to thirty victims in 1604) and this seriously jeopardised the livelihood of playwrights and performers alike. A new outbreak of plague began in 1592 at the end of Shakespeare's first phase of dramatic creativity and the playhouses were shut between 20 September and 8 December 1592 and 2 February 1593 and June 1594. Shakespeare seems to have survived this fallow period better than many by turning to poetry. In April 1593, the erotic love poem, *Venus and Adonis*, was published by Richard Field and its dedication to the Right Honourable Henry Wriothesley, Earl of Southampton and Baron of Titchfield, suggests that if he was not exactly moving in aristocratic circles, Shakespeare was now enjoying some contact with the court. The poem, which charts the attempted wooing of the adolescent Adonis by the lusty Goddess of Love, Venus, is a swift, humorous and occasionally bawdy narrative. This is no better illustrated than when, locking 'her lily fingers one in one', Venus clasps the reluctant Adonis in her arms:

VENVS AND ADONIS.

Fie,liueleſſe picture,cold,and ſenceleſſe ſtone,
Well painted idoll,image dull and dead,
Statüe contenting but the eye alone,
Thing like a man,but of no woman bred:
    Thou art no man,though of a mans complexion,
    For men will kiſſe euen by their owne direction.

This ſaid,impatience chokes her pleading tong,
And ſwelling paſſion doth prouoke a pauſe,
Red cheeks, and fierie eyes blaſe forth her wrong:
Being iudge in loue, ſhe cannot right her cauſe.
    And now ſhe weeps,& now ſhe faine wold ſpeake,
    And now her ſobs do her intendments breake.

Sometimes ſhe ſhakes her head,and then his hand,
Now gazeth ſhe on him,now on the ground;
Sometimes her armes infold him like a band,
She would,he will not in her armes be bound:
    And when from thence he ſtruggles to be gone,
    She locks her lillie fingers one in one.

Fondling, ſhe ſaith,ſince I haue hemd thee here
Within the circuit of this iuorie pale,
Ile be the parke,and thou ſhalt be my deare:
Feed where thou wilt,on mountaine,or in dale;
    Graze on my lips,and if thoſe hils be drie,
    Stray lower, where the pleaſant fountaines lye.
                                        Within

VENVS AND ADONIS.

Within this limit is reliefe inough,
Sweet bottome graſſe , and high delightfull plaine,
Round riſing hillocks,brakes obſcure,and rough,
To ſhelter thee from tempeſt, and from raine :
    Then be my deare, ſince I am ſuch a parke,
    No dog ſhall rouze thee,though a thouſand bark.

At this *Adonis* ſmiles as in diſdaine,
That in each cheeke appeares a prettie dimple;
Loue made thoſe hollowes,if himſelfe were ſlaine,
He might be buried in a tombe ſo ſimple,
    Foreknowing well, if there he came to lye,
    Why there loue liu'd,& there he could not die.

Theſe louely caues,theſe round inchanting pits,
Opend their mouthes to ſwallow *Venus* liking :
Being mad before, how doth ſhe now for wits ?
Strucke dead at firſt, what needs a ſecond ſtriking?
    Poore Queene of loue,in thine own law forlorne,
    To loue a cheeke that ſmiles at thee in ſcorne.

Now which way ſhall ſhe turne? what ſhall ſhe ſay?
Her words are done, her woes the more increaſing,
The time is ſpent,her obiect will away,
And from her twining armes doth vrge releaſing :
    Pitie ſhe cries,ſome fauour,ſome remorſe;
    Away he ſprings,and haſteth to his horſe.

Extract from the erotic love-poem Venus and Adonis *showing the determined attempt of the goddess to seduce the adolescent Adonis (l.222-240).*

British Library C.21.a.37

'Fondling', she saith, 'since I have hemm'd thee here

Within the circuit of this ivory pale,

I'll be a park, and thou shalt be my deer:

Feed where thou wilt, on mountain or in dale;

Graze on thy lips, and if those hills be dry,

Stray lower, where the pleasant fountains lie.

Within this limit is relief enough,

Sweet bottom grass and high delightful plain,

Round rising hillocks, brakes obscure and rough,
To shelter thee from tempest and from rain:
Then be my deer, since I am such a park,
No dog shall rouse thee, though a thousand bark.

(229-240)

The comedy of the pursuit, the frustration of the non-consummation and the tragedy of the ending (Venus is inconsolable when Adonis is killed by a boar when hunting) proved hugely popular with Elizabethan and Jacobean readers, and sixteen editions were published between 1593 and 1640. A second narrative poem, *The Rape of Lucrece*, was also a success, numbering eight editions from its publication in 1594 (with a second dedication to Wriothesley). Its subject matter, the rape of Lucrece by Tarquin, obviously demanded a more sober treatment, and in the urgency of its opening stanza -

From the besieged Ardea all in post,
Borne by the trustless wings of false desire,
Lust-breathed Tarquin leaves the Roman host
And to Collatium bears the lightless fire,
Which in pale embers hid, lurks to aspire,
And girdle with embracing flames the waist
Of Collatine's fair love, Lucrece the chaste.

(1-6)

- we can see some of the terror that would soon be apparent in the mature tragedies at the turn of the century.

❧ *The Lord Chamberlain's Men*

Shakespeare's New Company

The plague passed in the summer of 1594 and this was to prove a year of decisive importance for Shakespeare's career. In June a new company was formed under the patronage of Henry Carey, first Baron Hunsdon, who was Queen Elizabeth's Lord Chamberlain. On 8 October, 'the time being such as, thanks be to God, there is now no danger of the sickness', Hunsdon requested permission from the Lord Mayor of London to perform during the coming winter months at the Cross Keys Inn in Gracious Street. We have no firm evidence that Shakespeare was associated with the Lord Chamberlain's Men from their inception, but it seems a fair supposition. In any event, he is named on 15 March 1595 in the accounts of the treasurer of the Queen's Chamber as joint payee, along with William Kempe and Richard Burbage, for the performance of 'two several comedies or interludes' given before the queen the previous Christmas at Greenwich.

The advantages of being attached to a single company (and Shakespeare remained with this troupe for the rest of his career) were enormous, not least because he could write for a specific group of players and tailor his scripts according to their strengths and weaknesses. When the Lord Chamberlain's men moved into the Globe in 1599, he would be able to write with a permanent stage space in mind as well.

Sonnets

The first four years of the existence of the Lord Chamberlain's Men - 1594-8 - were a time of professional enhancement, personal wealth and private tragedy for Shakespeare. Frances Meres' *Wit's Treasury* (1598) provides further testimony of the playwright's growing reputation. 'The sweet, witty soul of Ovid lives in mellifluous and honey-tongued Shakespeare', Meres observes, 'witness his *Venus and Adonis*, his Lucrece, his sugared sonnets among his private friends'. This reference to the private circulation of the sonnets is fascinating, since they were not actually published until 1609 and have long been considered the most autobiographical of all

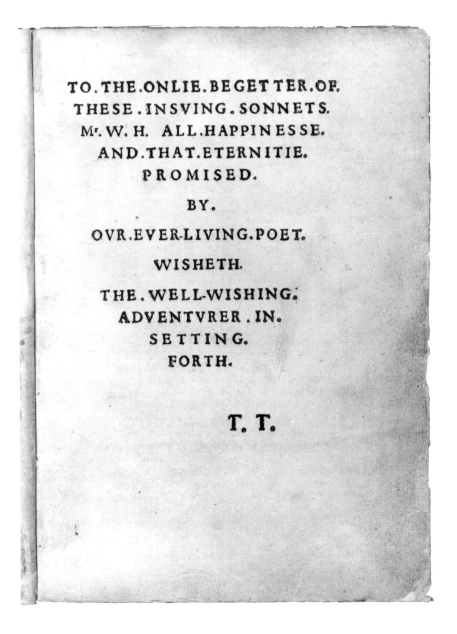

Shakespeare's writing. The danger of reading the sonnets as if the 'I' of the poet persona *is* actually Shakespeare cannot be overestimated, because there is no proof that they were devised to express personal emotions, but the range of their subject matter and the intensity of their feeling suggest a strong degree of authorial engagement. Although there is no narrative thread to the 154 poems in the collection, there are a number of recurring themes. The bulk of the poems are addressed to a beautiful young man and range over many topics. In the first 18 sonnets, for example, the poet is obsessed with the notion of transience and urges the young man to recognise the ravaging effects of time, which can only be defeated by the birth of a child (once again, the era's obsession with procreation is apparent). 'When I do count the clock that tells the time' (No.12) and 'Shall I compare thee to a summer's day' (No.18) belong to this group. Some of the sonnets are so intense that it is hard not to question whether they were inspired by personal feelings. For example, sonnet 29 addresses the pain of public disgrace ('I all alone beweep my outcast sight') which is mitigated by the 'sweet love' of the youth; sonnets 40, 41 and 42 express the fiercely jealous feelings of the poet at the rival attraction for the youth of a mysterious woman (the so-called 'Dark Lady') -

> *Take all my loves, my love, yea, take them all;*
> *What hast thou then more than thou hadst before?*
>
> (40 : 1 – 2)

Sonnet 57 reveals the slavery of the poet to his passion and sonnet 61 laments the insomnia that swiftly follows ('Two loves I have, of comfort and despair'); and sonnet 147 describes love as a sickness that must be experienced ('My love is as a fever') and reflects on the tantalising nature of the Dark Lady -

> *For I have sworn thee fair, and thought thee bright,*
> *Who art as black as hell, as dark as night.*
>
> (147 : 13 – 14)

Ultimately, the beautifully crafted and frequently disturbing fourteen-line poems pose biographical questions that cannot be answered. The identity of Mr W.H., to whom the 1609 edition is dedicated; the names of the youth, Dark Lady and rival poet - if they existed at all; and the extent to which the poems reflect Shakespeare's own psyche, are all destined to remain hidden. One event of great personal distress to Shakespeare did take place, however, in 1596. His only son, Hamnet, died age 11 and was buried on 11 August in Stratford. Was this the event that made him speculate so intensely on procreation, posterity and permanence?

SONNETS.

10

FOr shame deny that thou bear'st loue to any
Who for thy selfe art so vnprouident
Graunt if thou wilt, thou art belou'd of many,
But that thou none lou'st is most euident:
For thou art so possest with murdrous hate,
That gainst thy selfe thou stickst not to conspire,
Seeking that beautious roofe to ruinate
Which to repaire should be thy chiefe desire:
O change thy thought, that I may change my minde,
Shall hate be fairer log'd then gentle loue?
Be as thy presence is gracious and kind,
Or to thy selfe at least kind harted proue,
    Make thee an other selfe for loue of me,
    That beauty still may liue in thine or thee.

11

AS fast as thou shalt wane so fast thou grow'st,
In one of thine, from that which thou departest,
And that fresh bloud which yongly thou bestow'st,
Thou maist call thine, when thou from youth conuertest,
Herein liues wisdome, beauty, and increase,
Without this follie, age, and could decay,
If all were minded so, the times should cease,
And threescoore yeare would make the world away:
Let those whom nature hath not made for store,
Harsh, featurelesse, and rude, barrenly perrish,
Looke whom she best indow'd, she gaue the more;
Which bountious guift thou shouldst in bounty cherrish,
    She caru'd thee for her seale, and ment therby,
    Thou shouldst print more, not let that coppy die.

12

VVHen I doe count the clock that tels the time,
And see the braue day suncke in hidious night,
When I behold the violet past prime,
And sable curls or siluer'd ore with white:
When lofty trees I see barren of leaues,
Which erst from heat did canopie the herd

B3   And

SHAKE-SPEARES

And Sommers greene all girded vp in sheaues
Borne on the beare with white and bristly beard:
Then of thy beauty do I question make
That thou among the wastes of time must goe,
Since sweets and beauties do them-selues forsake,
And die as fast as they see others grow,
    And nothing gainst Times sieth can make defence
    Saue breed to braue him, when he takes thee hence.

13

O That you were your selfe, but loue you are
No longer yours, then you your selfe here liue,
Against this cumming end you should prepare,
And your sweet semblance to some other giue.
So should that beauty which you hold in lease
Find no determination, then you were
You selfe again after your selfes decease,
When your sweet issue your sweet forme should beare.
Who lets so faire a house fall to decay,
Which husbandry in honour might vphold,
Against the stormy gusts of winters day
And barren rage of deaths eternall cold?
    O none but vnthrifts, deare my loue you know,
    You had a Father, let your Son say so.

14

NOt from the stars do I my iudgement plucke,
And yet me thinkes I haue Astronomy,
But not to tell of good, or euil lucke,
Of plagues, of dearths, or seasons quallity,
Nor can I fortune to breefe mynuits tell;
Pointing to each his thunder, raine and winde,
Or say with Princes if it shal go wel
By oft predict that I in heauen finde,
But from thine eies my knowledge I deriue,
And constant stars in them I read such art
As truth and beautie shal together thriue
If from thy selfe, to store thou wouldst conuert:

Or

'Shakespeare...is the most excellent'

Wit's Treasury also contained a useful checklist of plays that Shakespeare had written up to 1598. 'As Plautus and Seneca are accounted best for comedy and tragedy among the Latins', Meres wrote

> so Shakespeare among the English is the most excellent in both kinds for the stage; for comedy, witness his **Gentlemen of Verona**, his **Errors**, his **Love's Labour's Lost**, his **Love's Labour's Won**, his **Midsummer Night's Dream**, and his **Merchant of Venice**; for tragedy, his **Richard the Second**, **Richard the Third**, **Henry the Fourth**, **King John**, **Titus Andronicus**, and his **Romeo and Juliet**.

Sonnets 10-13.

British Library C.21.e.44

Opposite page:

*Arendt van Buchel's
drawing from
Johannes de Witt's
sketch of the Swan
playhouse, made in
1595. Note the
spectators behind the
stage, the size of the
columns and the space
beneath the acting area
to permit concealment.*

Utrecht University Library

Meres' list reveals that one of Shakespeare's plays has been subsequently lost - *Love's Labour's Won* (what price a re-discovered manuscript?) - and that since the formation of the Lord Chamberlain's Men, he had written five more plays: *The Comedy of Errors* (*c.*1593-4), *Richard II* (*c.*1595), *Henry IV Parts One* (*c.*1596) and *Part Two* (*c.*1597) and *The Merchant of Venice* (*c.*1597).

Just as the trilogy of *Henry VI* plays and *Richard III* belonged chronologically together, so do *Richard II* and the two parts of *Henry IV*. Richard II was a problematic figure for Elizabethan England, since he was a king who had been deposed in 1399. The usurper was the Duke of Hereford, Henry Bolingbroke, who afterwards became Henry IV. This posed a dilemma for Shakespeare. On the one hand, the usurpation of the rightful monarch was one of the ultimate heresies for Tudor England, but on the other, it had actually been necessary for Henry IV to accede to the throne to ensure the eventual succession of Elizabeth I. The situation was further complicated by the analogies that were sometimes drawn by Elizabeth's courtiers (not necessarily unfavourably) between the queen and the unfortunate king. In his second history cycle, Shakespeare attempts to have his cake and eat it. On the debit side, Richard is seen as being guilty of complicity in the murder of the Duke of Gloucester; his wars in Ireland and the taxes levied to fund them are bleeding England dry; he is surrounded by flatterers (the 'caterpillars of the commonwealth'); and he lacks the judgement and common touch of Bolingbroke. However, as Richard's fortunes wane, our sympathy for him rises. By the end of the play, his isolation takes on a tragic dimension. He reminds us of his divine right -

*Not all the water in the rough rude sea
Can wash the balm off from an anointed king*

(III ii 54-5)

- he rightly predicts the endless wars between rival houses that would overshadow the coming reigns (and in Tudor historiography would not be calmed until Elizabeth's reign); and his eventual death is seen as a cruel, squalid act, given his naming of Bolingbroke as his heir. No wonder that the new king vows to

RICARDVS II

make a voyage to the Holy Land,

To wash this blood off from my guilty hand.

(V vi 49-50)

Henry IV's guilt, however, is not really expiated in the two plays that bear his name. Constantly tormented by remembrance of his action, he is equally troubled by the behaviour of his son, Hal, who initially prefers the riotous companionship of Falstaff to the responsibilities of royal rank. These two plays are also about kingship, and, in particular, what an individual needs to sacrifice from his personality to become a respected ruler. On a personal level, Hal's rejection of Falstaff in *Part Two* seems cruel and ungrateful. On a national level, it is a necessary action to allow him to put personal pleasure before public duty and become the dynamic and inspirational ruler

Opposite page:

King Richard II, (born 1367, crowned 1377, died 1400) painted by an unknown artist.

National Portrait Gallery

Left:

The Earl of Essex. Painted by Nicholas Hillard, 1547 – 1619.

National Portrait Gallery

of *Henry V*. It is a lesson of which Elizabeth I would have thoroughly approved.

There is a coda to *Richard II* which reveals a unique after-life for an Elizabethan work. The published Quarto version of the play omitted the deposition scene, possibly on orders from the censor, and the queen's own sense of a link between herself and Richard II was articulated when she told William Lambarde on 4 August 1601, 'I am Richard II, know ye not that?'. Her insecurity was heightened by the attempted rebellion staged by her former favourite, the Earl of Essex, earlier in that same year. The day before he launched his uprising on 8 February 1601, some of his followers had paid the Lord Chamberlain's Men forty shillings to stage a play at the Globe that was described by one of the Globe shareholders, Augustine Phillips, as being 'so old and so long out of use that they should have small or no company at it. But at their request [they] were content to play it.' Significantly, this long neglected play was *Richard II.*

The performance, however, did not rally Essex's troops. The rebellion failed, the players were quickly exonerated from any treasonable design and Essex was eventually executed for his disloyalty - the clearest example we have of the intertwining of art and life during Shakespeare's career.

As the playwright's portfolio of works grew, so did his personal fortune. In 1596 the College of Heralds finally granted John Shakespeare a coat-of-arms, depicting a shield crossed with a spear and surmounted by a falcon. He had officially been granted the status of a gentleman. Given his own decline in prosperity and the considerable fees that this would have required, it seems likely that the application had been made on John's behalf by his son, who was now a wealthy man. In 1597, William purchased the second largest house in Stratford, New Place and by 1598 he was storing grain in his new barns. Civic documents reveal that only two residents of the Chapel Street ward in Stratford could lay claim to more of the foodstuff.

In this early era of capitalism, Shakespeare flourished. Such was his new-found wealth that Richard Quiney, whose son Thomas was to marry his daughter Judith in 1616, asked him - in the only surviving letter addressed to Shakespeare - for a loan of £30. Although we do not know whether the loan was granted, we do know that this was a significant sum: the eminent Shakespearean scholar Stanley

Wells estimates that it would have paid the salary of the Stratford schoolmaster for eighteen months.

Shakespeare's knowledge of trade, commercial transactions and money-lending is evident in *The Merchant of Venice*. John Shakespeare had twice been accused in 1570 of breaking usury laws by making loans of £80 and £100 to Walter Musshem and of charging £20 interest on both sums, so both father and son had been more intimately connected to Shylock's trade than might be commonly thought. Of course, today's interest in the play reflects twentieth-century concerns: is the work anti-Semitic in its treatment of Shylock (who resolutely demands his 'pound of flesh' cut from Antonio's body as the agreed price for Antonio defaulting on his loan) and is Antonio's concern for Bassanio evidence of a homosexual love? It is arguable, however, that the play's examination of trade, natural justice and mercy were more compelling themes for an Elizabethan audience eager to make money, learn of new countries and steer clear of prohibitive laws.

The Birth of the Globe

By the end of the 1590s Shakespeare had become embedded in the theatrical life of London. He was a prolific playwright, with his two most recent works *The Merry Wives of Windsor* (c.1597) and *Much Ado About Nothing* (c.1598) testifying to his breathtaking speed of composition. He was a member of a company who performed regularly at Court - by the winter of 1596-7, all six of the Royal Command performances were given by the Lord Chamberlain's Men. He was a popular poet, on account of *Venus and Adonis* and *The Rape of Lucrece*, and he was still an occasional player (he features in the list of principal comedians who acted Ben Jonson's *Every Man in His Humour* in 1598). But two things clouded the horizon: a renewed attack by the Lord Mayor and Aldermen on playgoing in general, and the lack of a permanent venue for the Lord Chamberlain's Men in which to rehearse and perform.

In 1597, the Earl of Pembroke's Men performed a new play by Thomas Nashe and Ben Jonson at the Swan. The text of *The Isle of Dogs* is now lost, but its criticism of the government and the City of London was such that the Lord Mayor complained in July to the Privy Council. Following an investigation by the Middlesex Justices into the 'lewd plaie that was plaied in one of the plaiehouses on the Bancke Side,

contanynge very seditious and scandalous matter' , Jonson and several members of Pembroke's Men were imprisoned. Even more serious for public theatre as a whole was the Privy Council's subsequent order that seemed to threaten the curtailment of public drama:

> *Her Majestie being informed that there are verie great disorders committed in the common playhouses both by lewd matters that are handled on the stages and by resorte and confluence of bad people, hathe given direction that not onlie no plaies shalbe used within London or about the city or in any publique place during this tyme of sommer, but that also those playhouses that are erected and built only for suche purposes shalbe plucked downe.*

Actually, as critic Peter Thomson has pointed out, the order had the effect of reorganising rather than eradicating public drama. It seems that the Privy Council intended that aristocratic patronage should be confined to two companies - the Lord Admiral's Men and the Lord Chamberlain's - and it may have been this that finally galvanised Shakespeare's company into seeking out a permanent venue. Also, the continuing pleasure that Elizabeth herself took in Court performances (and the subsequent enthusiasm of James I) provided useful protection and led to the concession that that theatre companies should be able to rehearse in public for performances in the royal palaces. The 1597 order did, however, initiate a trend towards a more court-based drama that accelerated during the Stuart dynasty.

In the aftermath of this order Shakespeare's company moved to consolidate its position. James Burbage, the pioneering builder of The Theatre, died in February 1597 and left the property to his younger son, Richard. Richard was one of the six shareholders of the Lord Chamberlain's Men (the others being Thomas Pope, Augustine Phillips, William Kempe, John Heminges

Opposite page:

Ben Jonson, playwright (1572/3-1637), painted c.1617 by Abraham von Blyenberch (fl.1617-1622).

National Portrait Gallery

Below:

Portrait of Richard Burbage, actor (c.1567-1619), by an unknown artist.

Dulwich Picture Gallery

and William Shakespeare) and he seemed to have inherited a ready-made permanent home for the company. However, the situation was complicated by the fact that the lease on the land was due to expire in 1598, and although there was a clause in James Burbage's original lease that permitted the tenant to dismantle and relocate the building, it was unclear whether this was legally enforceable after the lease had expired. In autumn 1598, the new lessee, Giles Allen, refused to renegotiate terms, so the company took matters into its own hands. On 28 December 1598, Richard Burbage, his mother, brother, financial backer William Smith, carpenter and architect Peter Street and several labourers began to dismantle The Theatre during the night. It was a bitterly cold evening and the Thames was frozen - it may have been that they actually slid the timbers across the river to their destination on Bankside, only two hundred metres from the Rose theatre that was managed by their great rival, Philip Henslowe. On 21 February 1599 a new agreement was signed, with the owner of the land, Nicholas Brend, conveying half the lease to Richard and Cuthbert Burbage, and the other half to Pope, Phillips, Heminges, Kempe and Shakespeare. The most famous theatre in

The Gallery in the reconstructed Globe Theatre, Bankside, London.

Tiffany Foster, Shakespeare's Globe

the world, the Globe, had been born, and would be ready for performances in the autumn of 1599. By joining the new breed of theatre entrepreneurs, Shakespeare, as writer, player and shareholder, had become a total man of the theatre.

Stage Conditions at the Globe

What was it like to watch a performance of a Shakespeare play at the Globe? Recent historical research, not least that emerging from productions at the splendid reconstructed playhouse on London's South Bank, has supplied us with a fair idea. The Globe season began in late August and continued up to Christmas. During the seasonal celebrations, the Lord Chamberlain's Men would hope to be invited to court to perform indoors and for a large fee before the monarch. For this, they could expect to receive £10, a much greater sum than the receipts of one Globe performance. It is likely that, in spite of the inclement weather, performances would have continued back at the Globe from January until the beginning of Lent, during which time playing became more intermittent. Once Lent was over, spring-time performances would recommence and continue until the arrival of summer, when the flies and lice that helped spread the plague made both performing and spectating unbearable. Consequently, in July and August (and possibly earlier depending on epidemics) the company went on tour to the provinces (Henslowe records the purchase of a drum for 11*s* 6*d* for his company's excursion into the country in 1599).

Performances began at 2pm in the winter and 4pm in the summer. Spectators could pay a penny to stand in the yard, a further penny to sit in the first gallery and one penny more to sit in the second. The atmosphere in the yard was like the stadium of a football match. The most prestigious seating was in the Lord's Box, above and behind the stage, where dignitaries could observe and be observed in equal measure.

Since there were no lights to dim or curtains to raise, playwrights utilised a variety of devices to secure the attention of the audience at the beginning of the play. The hoisting of the flag above the theatre was probably not sufficient in itself, so Shakespeare at the beginning of *Henry V* has a Chorus appeal directly to the audience to allow their imagination to be acted upon by what they see:

O for a muse of fire, that would ascend
The brightest heaven of invention,
A Kingdom for a stage, princes to act,
And monarchs to behold the swelling scene!

(Prologue : 1 – 4)

Although *Henry V* is likely to have had its first performance at the Curtain theatre in 1599, Shakespeare was clearly thinking about the work being performed in the new venue, since the Chorus continues by asking

Can this cockpit hold
The vasty fields of France? Or may we cram
Within this wooden O the very casques
That did affright the air at Agincourt?

(Prologue : 1 – 4)

It is as if the playwright is already speculating about the unknown potential of the new space.

As You Like It (*c.*1599) begins with a long speech by Orlando in mid-conversation with Adam and this indicates that audiences did not necessarily need a dramatic jolt to settle down. This play is likely to have been the first performed at the Globe and Jacques's famous speech, 'All the world's a stage', is particularly apt, since the inscription on the Globe's sign expresses a similar sentiment: *Totus Mundus Agit Histrionem* ('The Whole World moves the Actor'), with Hercules depicted carrying the world on his shoulders. Even the very name of the Globe testifies to the expansive ambitions of the late Elizabethan age.

Given the close proximity of the audience to the stage, the numbers that could be crammed in (incredibly, as many as 2000) and the intimate nature of the environment, the temptation for the players to interact

The reconstructed Globe, Bankside, London.

Tiffany Foster, Shakespeare's Globe

directly with the spectators must have been enormous. Peter Thomson has calculated that since there was always a phenomenal turnover of plays (in the first two weeks of September 1595, for example, the Admiral's Men performed ten different plays), rehearsal time could, at most, have totalled 24 hours - enough to have ensured the mastering of tricky stage business and the recollection of lines, but little else. Individual players would have been given scripts that merely contained their own lines and a prompt, and it is possible that only the prompter ever possessed a complete copy of the play. To rehearse and produce *Hamlet* in twenty-four hours seems incredible by today's standards but whilst this would have restricted a psychological approach to performance, it might have meant that spontaneous interaction with an audience and the use of improvisation would have been actively encouraged: the booing of a wicked prince, or shared enjoyment of a joke, for example. Shakespeare took no care to publish his work during his lifetime and the pre-eminence of the text today is something that Elizabethans would have found incomprehensible.

A performance at the reconstructed Globe, Bankside, London.

Tiffany Foster, Shakespeare's Globe

With little time to rehearse, there was little opportunity or taste for scenery. A bench or a screen might be carried on through the two doors at the back of the stage, but this was predominantly a theatre of illusion, where the stage was frequently empty but for the players. A series of conventions must therefore have emerged that governed the reception of the performance. For example, audiences must have accepted that a soliloquy could be audible to them but inaudible to others on stage. Equally, characters could be visible to spectators but invisible to each other, and entrances were generally announced before they were made.

Shakespeare quickly came to write with this specific stage space in mind. The two pillars that supported the tiring house (which contained pulleys and other machinery above the stage) offered scope for concealment, as did a curtain strung up between them. Therefore, we begin to see from now on a proliferation of scenes where characters eavesdrop on each other (for example, the conspirators in *Julius Caesar*, Iago listening to Othello), use the space behind the pillars as a second chamber (Hamlet stabbing Polonius through the arras) or integrate the tiring house itself into the action (Cleopatra hauling up the dying Antony into her monument).

Julius Caesar (c.1599) is the first of Shakespeare's plays which we can confidently state was performed at the Globe, since a Swiss visitor to London, Thomas Platter, records that he attended a production of it in September 1599:

> *After dinner on the 21st of September, at about two o'clock, I went with my companions over the water, and in the strewn roof-house saw the tragedy of the first Emperor Julius with at least fifteen characters very well acted. At the end of the comedy they danced according to their custom, with extreme elegance. Two in men's clothes and two in women's gave this performance, in wonderful combination with each other.*

The work is an interesting reflection of the current uncertainty surrounding the realm as the queen became increasingly frail, and the matter of succession still seemed unresolved. Indeed, it deals with the assassination of the legitimate ruler of Rome and charts the price that the assassins have to pay for their crime. Brutus might be acting from the most honourable of motives, but the deposition of the imperious but legitimate, Julius Caesar, ushers in civil strife and much bloodshed and ends with both Brutus and Cassius committing suicide with the dead Emperor's name on their lips. Better the status quo than uncertain rebellion over the question of the succession, Shakespeare seems to be saying.

Extract from Hamlet *in the First Folio showing the 'To be, or not to be' speech (III I 56-89).*

British Library C.39.k.15

In this light, *Hamlet* (*c*.1600/1), too, seems to have much to say about kingship - this time highlighting the dangers of an elective monarchy - but our interest in the play today is based on other grounds. The work has probably become the most famous play of all time. The ultimate Revenge Tragedy, full of intellectual and philosophical enquiry, it deals with the anguish that young Hamlet feels on discovering that his father had been murdered and that his mother had married the murderer, Claudius. Its appeal is probably rooted in the fact that although Hamlet is a prince, his hesitation in acting against Claudius, examining all the moral implications of a potential murder, is a character trait with which we can all identify. The work is also compellingly theatrical - be it in the supernatural appearance of his father's Ghost, the assumption of Hamlet's 'antic disposition' where he appears to go mad or the tragic relationship between the prince and Ophelia - and the role has now become one of the ultimate challenges for any actor. That it was written close to the death of Shakespeare's own father, John, in 1601 and that his only son had been called Hamnet adds some biographical colour to the play.

The text of *Hamlet* highlights the difficulties that modern editors face in establishing the precise version that Shakespeare himself created. On 26 July 1602, an edition, known now as Q1 (the first quarto), was entered in the Stationers Register. It contains 2154 lines and is generally viewed as a version reconstructed by one of the original actors, although recently scholars, such as Eric Sams, have challenged the plausibility of this theory. In 1604, a second edition, styling itself as 'the true and perfect Coppie' and now known as Q2, was printed. It is much longer, at 3723 lines, and is generally felt to be closer to the original manuscript, but the Folio edition of 1623 seems to be based on yet another manuscript (although it shows links to Q2), leaving a very tricky editorial decision. Which sections of which version actually constitute Shakespeare's original thoughts? Here is another reason not to become too obsessed with textual fidelity.

Shakespeare's final plays of Elizabeth's reign were *Twelfth Night* (*c*.1600), which was probably performed at court on 6 January 1601, *Troilus and Cressida* (*c*.1602) and *All's Well That Ends Well* (*c*.1603). The Lord Chamberlain's Men had acquired a new clown, Robert Armin, and the role of Malvolio in *Twelfth Night* is likely to have been written with him in mind.

Elizabeth's reign certainly did end well for Shakespeare, since, above all, the Globe was proving a profitable business concern. In spite of the money that was occasionally lavished on costume (Henslowe records the expense of £9 for taffeta to make women's gowns for *The Two Angry Women of Abington*, against box office takings of £3) and the the fees paid to the Master of the Revels for licensing new works (9 shillings), the Globe earned Shakespeare and the five other shareholders large sums of money. Such was his income that Shakespeare was able to pay, on 1 May 1602, £320 in cash for 107 acres of arable land in Old Stratford, as well as purchasing in the same year a cottage and garden in Chapel Lane, opposite his own garden in New Place. In his private life, too, he seemed to be enjoying the fruits of his labours, as this rare insight, recorded by the London law student, John Manningham, in 1602 confirms:

> *Upon a time when Burbage played Richard III there was a citizen grew so far in liking with him that, before she went from the play, she appointed him to come that night unto her by the name of Richard the Third. Shakespeare, overhearing their conclusion, went before, was entertained, and at his game ere Burbage came. Then, message being brought that Richard the Third was at the door, Shakespeare caused return to be made that William the Conqueror was before Richard the Third.*

The question now remained: would Shakespeare continue to flourish under a new monarch whose reign marked the end of the Tudors and the beginning of the Stuarts?

James I and Jacobean England to 1616

King of Scotland

James acceded to the Scottish throne at the age of one when his mother, Mary Queen of Scots, abdicated, following her defeat by rebel Scottish lords. A year later, in 1568, Mary fled to England and her son never saw his mother again. The young James VI received an education in the classics, theology and French literature and he soon began to impress his subjects with his great knowledge. He enjoyed hunting, wrote poetry and quickly exhibited a deep desire for peace, which remained with him all his life, and, although a convinced Presbyterian, he never sought to impose this English religious creed on his Scottish subjects. Such political tact was less in evidence when he became the King of England.

In 1587, Elizabeth I reluctantly consented to the execution of Mary Queen of Scots but, ever eager to remain on harmonious terms with Elizabeth so as not to imperil his own claim to the throne, James restricted himself to a formal protest. James's love life exercises fascination today because he was evidently a bisexual monarch. His marriage, when he was twenty-three, to Anne, the daughter of Frederick II of Denmark, produced two sons (Prince Henry in 1594 and Prince Charles, later Charles I, in 1600), but by 1604 he had ceased marital relations with the queen. Although he shared her interest in masques and pageantry, he disliked her Roman Catholicism, and increasingly came to enjoy the company of his own sex. He managed to remain on cordial terms with his wife, however.

Two works that were written by James, *Daemonologie* (1597) and *Basilikon Doron* (1599), testify to his fear of the spirit world, his vivid belief in the power of the devil and his conviction that the king was appointed to the throne by God and ruled through 'divine right'. This self-confidence, which Elizabeth shared but expressed with a surer touch, was to cause great difficulties between James and the English parliament.

The ground for James's eventual succession - a subject that had so terrified the English during the 1590s - was prepared by Sir Robert Cecil, Elizabeth's chief minister, during the final years of her life. As a direct descendant of Henry VII's daughter, Margaret Tudor, James had the strongest claim (*see page 11*), and Cecil began a secret correspondence with James in March 1601, urging him not to divulge the nature of their preparations, since 'if Her Majesty had known all I did...her age and orbit, joined to the jealousy of her sex, might have moved her to think ill of that which helped preserve her.'

When the Elizabethan age finally came to an end with the death of the queen at 3.00 am on 24 March 1603, arrangements for the succession were all in place. The text of a proclamation of James's accession was approved by the Privy Councillors barely three hours later, and then read out at Whitehall Gate and at a carefully staged ceremony at the Cross in Cheapside. Cecil himself proclaimed James to be the 'King of England, France and Ireland, Defender of the Faith'.

The peaceful nature of this transition of power was such that although James did not travel down to London until May on account of an outbreak of plague, the new king enjoyed a brief honeymoon period with a greatly relieved populace. His ending of the wars with Spain in 1604 brought further gratitude, but the difficulties to come were evident at the Hampton Court Conference in the same year, which had been convened to discuss matters of religion. Both the Puritans and the Catholics had been hopeful of securing concessions from the new king, but both were to be disappointed. The Puritans reacted by proceeding to consolidate their power in parliament, thereby sowing the seeds of the dissension that would ultimately plunge the country into civil war. The Catholics, on the other hand, took more immediate action. A conspiracy was hatched, aimed at blowing up the king, the queen and the young Prince Henry on 5 November 1605 in the House of Parliament, and it was only by chance that the potential regicide was discovered at the last minute. The unmasking of Robert Catesby and Guy Fawkes's plot and the subsequent hysteria that this provoked inevitably intensified the bitter suspicion of the Protestants against the Catholics. This led to a rigorous enforcement of the recusancy laws, which fined those who refused to attend Protestant services. These laws had been less strictly applied

Guy Fawkes (detail from the illustration on page 77).

William Shakespeare

*King James VI
of Scotland,
later King James I
of England (born 1566,
crowned King of
England 1603,
died 1626),
painted by
an unknown artist.*

CONCILIVM SEPTEM NOBILIVM ANGLORVMCONIVRANTIVM JN NECEM IACOBI·I·
MAGNÆ· BRITANNIÆ· REGIS TOTIVSQ· ANGLICI· CONVOCATI PARLEMENTI·

Bates · Robert Winter · Christopher Wright · Iohn Wright · Thomas Percy · Guido Fawkes · Robert Catesby · Thomas Winter

under Elizabeth, as indicated by the fact that John Shakespeare had been listed as a recusant in 1592.

The Gunpowder Plotters, 1605.

National Portrait Gallery

James brought further difficulties upon himself by undertaking a succession of measures that alienated many of his subjects. Whereas Elizabeth had demonstrated her common touch with regular processions throughout her kingdom, James appeared aloof and remote, preferring to remain in his palaces. The people of Scotland had marvelled at his supposed intellect, but his English subjects were more distracted by his spindly legs and his narrow jaws, which made eating difficult. As public revenues fell and prices rose, James - who had little money sense - sought to generate income through the dubious practice of selling knighthoods, and ultimately baronetcies, which led to the public perception of cronyism at the heart of the court. In Ben Jonson's *The Devil is an Ass* (1616) even the devil is staggered by the immorality that he discovers in the capital. The king's increasing reliance on favourites, such as the Duke of Buckingham, left parliament feeling alienated and the population confused. By the time of James's death in 1625, the realm was in a sorry state - riven by factions, threatened by Spain with renewed conflict and financially distressed.

The Hampton Court Conference did have one beneficial result, the eventual publication in 1611 of a new translation of the Bible, known as the King James version. This magnificent work with its beautiful prose style provides a useful reminder that the early part of James's reign, that which takes us to Shakespeare's death in 1616, was a period not without success. In the arts, in particular, James was to prove a valuable patron, and one of his first acts on becoming king was to announce in letters patent on 19 May 1603 that the former Lord Chamberlain's Men would henceforward be known as the King's Men:

> *Knowe yee that Wee of our speciall grace, certeine knowledge, & mere motion have licenced and aucthorized and by theise presentes doe licence and aucthorize theise our Servauntes Lawrence Fletcher, William Shakespeare, Richard Burbage, Augustyne Phillippes, Iohn Heninges, Henrie Condell, William Sly, Robert Armyn, Richard Cowly, and the rest of theire Assosiates freely to vse and exercise the Arte and faculty of playinge Comedies, Tragedies, histories, Enterludes, moralls, pastoralls, Stage-plaies, and Suche others like as theie haue alreadie studied or hereafter shall vse or studie, aswell for the recreation of our lovinge Subjectes, as for our Solace and pleasure when wee shall thincke good to see them, duringe our pleasure.*

The patent also defined their newly confirmed rights:

> *to shewe and exercise publiquely to their best Commoditie, when the infection of the plague shall decrease, aswell within theire nowe vsual howse called the Globe within our County of Surrey, as alsoe within anie towne halls or Moute halls or other conveniente places within the liberties and freedome of anie other Cittie, vniversitie, towne, or Boroughe whatsoever within our said Realmes and domynions.*

Shakespeare could not have aquired a more powerful patron and the company was now confirmed as the pre-eminent theatrical troupe in the country. The transition from the patronage of one monarch to another had been effortless.

The King's Men

The King's Playwright?

As Queen Elizabeth was taken ill for the last time in 1603, the theatres were closed on 19 March as a mark of respect. They re-opened on 24 March but were soon compelled to close again on 26 May as the number of plague deaths rapidly rose. The theatres were to remain shut for eleven months, by which time almost 30,000 Londoners (out of a total population of 200,000) had succumbed to the epidemic. The King's Men presumably went on tour to the provinces during this period and we know that Shakespeare, perhaps temporarily on account of the closure of the playhouses, resumed his career as an actor. The cast list of Ben Jonson's *Sejanus His Fall* includes his name.

During the Christmas and Shrovetide celebrations of 1603, the King's Men were commanded to perform in front of the king no fewer than seven times, and their proximity to the centre of power was confirmed when they were invited to participate in the celebrations surrounding the signing of the peace treaty with Spain in 1604, by entertaining the Spanish Ambassador, Juan Fernandez de Velasco, at Somerset House. But even though four of Shakespeare's own works were performed at court in 1604 (*Othello* (1 November), *The Merry Wives of Windsor* (4 November), *Measure for Measure* (26 December), *The Comedy of Errors* (28 December)), it would be a mistake to assume that Shakespeare was the king's own playwright, consistently reflecting the priorities and beliefs of the monarch. *Measure for Measure* (c.1604), for example, poses searching questions about the business of rule. Duke Vincentio's decision to disguise himself as a friar and travel around the city to discover more about the views and living conditions of his subjects initially seems a well-intentioned, if unorthodox, move. But we quickly learn that this is a dubious political experiment –

> Hence shall we see
> If power change purpose, what our seemers be.

> (I iii 53-4)

- and that the appointment of his Deputy, Angelo, to rule in his absence is an ill-conceived one, given Angelo's inflexible attitudes and hypocritical morality. Far from being a responsible act, Vincentio's disappearance comes to be seen as an abnegation of responsibility that attempts to mask poorly framed laws of his own making. Although he manages to return to save Claudio's life and Isabella's virtue through a series of barely plausible subterfuges, *Measure for Measure* ends on a note of deliberate irresolution. The final speech of the play concludes with the Duke asking Isabella to marry him -

> *Dear Isabel,*
> *I have a motion much imports your good;*
> *Whereto if you'll a willing ear incline,*
> *What's mine is yours, and what is yours is mine.*
> *So, bring us to our palace, where we'll show*
> *What's yet behind that's meet you all should know.*
> FINIS
>
> (V i 531-6)

- but Isabella does not respond, allowing many subsequent directors of the play to end the work on a note of dissatisfaction and putative rebellion. No wonder that critics have termed the work a 'problem play' - problematic to categorise.

Measure for Measure strikes a more reflective, darker note than is evident in many of Shakespeare's plays of the Elizabethan period, and it starts a trend for the Jacobean works. Between 1604 and 1608, he was to write what are generally described as the mature tragedies that juxtapose personal tragedy with national upheaval. We can only speculate whether events in his own life caused him to write works that were more serious and brooding. Whereas elsewhere in the theatre of the period, works that attempted to foster a national consciousness (such as Shakespeare's history cycles) gave way to Jacobean tragedies that traced the revenge that various malcontents sought to obtain in foreign (frequently Italian) courts, Shakespeare tended to avoid these studies of rapacious individualism and chose to set his dramas against a more panoramic background.

The Mature Tragedies

Shakespeare's next four works were four great tragedies. The part of Othello is likely to have been written for the company's great tragedian, Richard Burbage, but the star role in production often belongs to the actor who plays Iago. The Romantic poet Samuel Taylor Coleridge famously described Iago as being a 'motiveless malignity', but Iago himself believes that he has sufficient reason to seek revenge against his superior. At the very least he feels slighted for having been passed over for promotion in favour of Cassio and he is tortured by the rumours that Othello may have had an affair with his wife, Emilia -

> *I hate the Moor;*
> *And it is thought abroad that 'twixt my sheets*
> *He's done my office;*
>
> (I iii 384-6)

The true fascination - and terror - for an audience is the way that Iago, little by little, fashions his plot to bring down Othello. There is no grand scheme: Iago is the ultimate opportunist. By tricking Othello into doubting Desdemona's fidelity with the horrific consequence of her murder, Iago not only proves that suggestibility and insecurity are a fatal combination, but that Othello's fate has fulfilled the very prophecy that the Moor himself did not heed:

> *O, beware, my lord, jealousy!*
> *It is the green-ey'd monster, which doth mock*
> *That meat it feeds on. That cuckold lives in bliss,*
> *Who, certain of his fate, loves not his wronger:*
> *But, O, what damned minutes tells he o'er*
> *Who dotes, yet doubts, suspects, yet strongly loves!*
>
> (III iii 169-74)

Extract from the First Folio showing the death of Lear and the unwillingess of those remaining to take up the reins of power at the end of the play. Act V iii 256pp.

British Library C.39.k.15

The Tragedie of King Lear.   309

If that her breath will mift or ftaine the ftone,
Why then fhe liues.
 Kent. Is this the promis'd end?
 Edg. Or image of that horror.
 Alb. Fall and ceafe.
 Lear. This feather ftirs, fhe liues: if it be fo,
It is a chance which do's redeeme all forrowes
That euer I haue felt.
 Kent. O my good Mafter.
 Lear. Prythee away.
 Edg. 'Tis Noble *Kent* your Friend.
 Lear. A plague vpon you Murderors, Traitors all,
I might haue fau'd her, now fhe's gone for euer:
Cordelia, Cordelia, ftay a little. Ha:
What is't thou faift? Her voice was euer foft,
Gentle, and low, an excellent thing in woman.
I kill'd the Slaue that was a hanging thee.
 Gent. 'Tis true (my Lords) he did.
 Lear. Did I not fellow?
I haue feene the day, with my good biting Faulchion
I would haue made him skip: I am old now,
And thefe fame croffes fpoile me. Who are you?
Mine eyes are not o'th beft, Ile tell you ftraight.
 Kent. If Fortune brag of two, fhe lou'd and hated,
One of them we behold.
 Lear. This is a dull fight, are you not *Kent?*
 Kent. The fame: your Seruant *Kent,*
Where is your Seruant *Caius?*
 Lear. He's a good fellow, I can tell you that,
He'le ftrike and quickly too, he's dead and rotten.
 Kent. No my good Lord, I am the very man.
 Lear. Ile fee that ftraight.
 Kent. That from your firft of difference and decay,
Haue follow'd your fad fteps.
 Lear. Your are welcome hither.
 Kent. Nor no man elfe:
All's cheerleffe, darke, and deadly,
Your eldeft Daughters haue fore-done themfelues,
And defperately are dead.
 Lear. I fo I thinke.
 Alb. He knowes not what he faies, and vaine is it

That we prefent vs to him.

    Enter a Meffenger.
 Edg. Very bootleffe.
 Meff. *Edmund* is dead my Lord.
 Alb. That's but a trifle heere:
You Lords and Noble Friends, know our intent,
What comfort to this great decay may come,
Shall be appli'd. For vs we will refigne,
During the life of this old Maiefty
To him our abfolute power, you to your rights,
With boote, and fuch addition as your Honours
Haue more then merited. All Friends fhall
Tafte the wages of their vertue, and all Foes
The cup of their deferuings : O fee, fee.
 Lear. And my poore Foole is hang'd: no, no, no life?
Why fhould a Dog, a Horfe, a Rat haue life,
And thou no breath at all? Thou'lt come no more,
Neuer, neuer, neuer, neuer, neuer.
Pray you vndo this Button. Thanke you Sir,
Do you fee this? Looke on her? Looke her lips,
Looke there, looke there.   *He dis.*
 Edg. He faints, my Lord, my Lord.
 Kent. Breake heart, I prythee breake.
 Edg. Looke vp my Lord.
 Kent. Vex not his ghoft, O let him paffe, he hates him,
That would vpon the wracke of this tough world
Stretch him out longer.
 Edg. He is gon indeed.
 Kent. The wonder is, he hath endur'd fo long,
He but vfurpt his life.
 Alb. Beare them from hence, our prefent bufineffe
Is generall woe : Friends of my foule, you twaine,
Rule in this Realme, and the gor'd ftate fuftaine.
 Kent. I haue a iourney Sir, fhortly to go,
My Mafter calls me, I muft not fay no.
 Edg. The waight of this fad time we muft obey,
Speake what we feele, not what we ought to fay :
The oldeft hath borne moft, we that are yong,
Shall neuer fee fo much, nor liue fo long.
     Exeunt with a dead March.
     ff 3

FINIS.

  Of all the tragedies, *King Lear* (1604/5) is the one that provokes the fiercest critical debate today. It has a rich plot. The elderly Lear wishes to divide up his kingdom amongst his three daughters, Goneril, Regan and Cordelia. The size of their portion will depend on the lavishness of their expression of love to him. Both Goneril and Regan shower him with insincere praise, but the youngest, Cordelia, who is Lear's favourite, refuses to participate in such a charade, and memorably chooses instead to say 'nothing'. Enraged, Lear banishes her to France and puts himself at the mercy of the seemingly more loyal elder sisters, but they view him as an irritant and eventually he leaves their homes to wander on the heath - tortured by both their inhumanity and a growing awareness of his injustice towards Cordelia. Accompanied by his Fool, who frequently acts as Lear's conscience, Lear wanders on the moor and becomes temporarily mad. Eventually, Cordelia and her husband, the King of France, land in Dover after the two sisters, squabbling over the bastard Edmund, have brought the country to its knees. A highly poignant reconciliation between Lear and Cordelia is effected, but this merely heightens the tragedy, since Edmund gives orders for Cordelia to be hanged and Lear, having brought her dead body onto the stage, dies of a broken heart.

Previously, scholars such as A.C. Bradley and E.M.W. Tillyard had argued that the tragedies demonstrated a belief in the natural order of things and that redemption was possible through suffering. For all the upheaval caused by the tragic hero succumbing to a fatal flaw (jealousy in Othello, for example), the promise of the restoration of order by the arrival of the new generation revealed that the tragedies were not entirely bleak. After all, Fortinbras represents hope for a new beginning at the end of *Hamlet* and Malcolm for a new dynasty at the climax of *Macbeth*. Recently however, this view has been challenged by academics such as Jonathan Dollimore and Kiernan Ryan, who counter that far from offering hope, the tragedies reflect a deep dissatisfaction with contemporary political structures and that the works are as critical of the Jacobean regime as was possible, given censorship and the necessary patronage that the monarch provided the King's Men. The battleground play for this debate is *King Lear*. Does the work simply represent a compelling personal tragedy? A 'fond, foolish old man' is only able to repent the division of his kingdom and the banishment of his favourite daughter, Cordelia, once he has temporarily gone mad, endured great suffering and affected a poignant reconciliation with this daughter, before she is brutally murdered by Edmund. According to this view Lear's own death from a broken heart brings about his personal redemption.

Or rather, is the work actually a savage critique of an ancient society (which may be a metaphor for Jacobean England), where a monarch is so unaccountable that he is able to divide up a kingdom with all its disastrous consequences; ruthless, amoral individuals such as Edmund, flourish; and the note of abject desolation struck when Lear carries onto the stage his dead daughter forces us to reflect on the type of society that has allowed this to happen?

The very last speech of the play is spoken by Edgar, Gloucester's son. Lear has died, Albany renounced his desire to rule and Kent refused to take up the reins of power, leaving a vacuum at the head of the country. When Edgar states that

The weight of this sad time we must obey;

Speak what we feel, not what we ought to say.

The oldest hath borne most: we that are young

Shall never see so much, nor live so long.

(V iii 323-6)

is this an expression of hope for the future uttered by one of the new generation, or, given the number of bodies (including Lear's and Cordelia's) on the stage, is this an invitation for the audience to ponder on how such a state of affairs could have been avoided? That the critical debate about this play is so fierce and unresolved is a specific example of the enduring power that Shakespeare possesses to intrigue and tantalise.

Shakespeare is less equivocal in *Macbeth* (1606), where equivocation - the use of ambiguous words in order to mislead - is a major theme. Of all his plays, it is the most sycophantic to James I and it again deals with an apparently loyal subject (the brave soldier Macbeth) murdering a legitimate ruler (Duncan). One of the main characters, Macbeth's friend Banquo, is a direct Scottish ancestor of the king and it is no accident that in the immediate aftermath of the murder of Duncan by Macbeth (having been goaded by his indomitable wife, Lady Macbeth), Shakespeare has Banquo declare, 'In the great hand of God I stand', emphasising his incorruptibility and handily touching on the notion of 'Divine Right'. In a similar vein, the witches, who encourage Macbeth in his murderous thoughts, tell Banquo that he is

Thunder. *Enter the three Witches.*

1 Thrice the brinded Cat hath mew'd.

2 Thrice, and once the Hedge-Pigge whin'd.

3 Harpier cries, 'tis time, 'tis time.

1 Round about the Caldron go:

In the poyfond Entrailes throw

Toad, that vnder cold ftone,

Dayes and Nights, ha's thirty one:

Sweltred Venom fleeping got,

Boyle thou firft i'th'charmed pot.

All. Double, double, toile and trouble;

Fire burne, and Cauldron bubble.

2 Fillet of a Fenny Snake,

In the Cauldron boyle and bake:

Eye of Newt, and Toe of Frogge,

Wooll of Bat, and Tongue of Dogge:

Adders Forke, and Blinde-wormes Sting,

Lizards legge, and Howlets wing:

For a Charme of powrefull trouble,

Like a Hell-broth, boyle and bubble.

All. Double, double, toyle and trouble,

Fire burne, and Cauldron bubble.

3 Scale of Dragon, Tooth of Wolfe,

Witches Mummey, Maw, and Gulfe

Of the rauin'd falt Sea fharke:

Roote of Hemlocke, digg'd i'th'darke:

Liuer of Blafpheming Iew,

Gall of Goate, and Slippes of Yew,

Sliuer'd in the Moones Ecclipfe:

Lesser than Macbeth, and greater.

Not so happy, yet much happier.

Thou shalt get kings, though thou be none.

(I iii 65-7)

and to clarify this prophecy of royal lineage, Macbeth sees on his second visit to the weird sisters 'A show of eight kings, the last with a glass in his hand; Banquo following'.

Further flattering strands include the play's depiction of the spirit world which touches on James's interest in demons (as expressed in his two books), its listing of the 'king-becoming graces' of

Justice, Verity, Temp'rance, Stableness,

Bounty, Perseverance, Mercy, Lowliness,

Devotion, Patience, Courage, Fortitude

(IV iii 92-4)

which could not have failed to please, and even the work's very length, which acknowledges the king's preference for short plays, articulated on a visit to Oxford in the summer of 1605. Of course, the main event that hangs over the entire work was the recently discovered Gunpowder Plot. The duplicity of the witches who 'lie like truth' echoes the nation's fear of Jesuit priests, whom it was believed had been granted absolution by the pope to use whatever means were necessary to bring about the death of James.

Macbeth's assassination of the saintly Duncan has dire consequences for the realms of both Scotland and England. His inability to desist from murder –

I am in blood

Stepp'd in so far, that, should I wade no more

Returning were as tedious as go o'er

(III iv 135-7)

– demonstrates both his own personal tragedy and the catastrophe that befalls the two kingdoms. His eventual demise at the hands of Macduff, who had been 'untimely ripp'd' from his mother's womb (born by caesarian section), demonstrates the fatal untrustworthiness of the witches, who had earlier stated that he would not be killed by a man 'of woman born'. Their duplicity is something that even Macbeth finally concedes -

> *be these juggling fiends no more believ'd ,*
> *That palter with us in a double sense.*

(V viii 19-20)

- and Macbeth's death is, in a sense, as necessary for Shakespeare's standing at court as it is for the play.

The final tragedy of this period, *Antony and Cleopatra* (1607-8), is the most wide-ranging of the entire canon. Returning to North's translation of Plutarch as his source (passages of which he was prepared to utilise almost word for word, such as Enobarbus's famous description of Cleopatra sitting in her barge), the play charts the unpredictable relationship between the exotic Queen of Egypt, Cleopatra, and the grizzled soldier of Rome, Antony. The play is built upon a series of opposites: the spaciousness of the world and the narrowness of a bed; the demands of love and the demands of the state; complete understanding of a partner alongside imperfect knowledge; extreme sensuality threatened by disdainful self-reserve; moments of great control juxtaposed against emotional disintegration; and military respect allied to personal antipathy. The concerns of the Elizabethan history plays have been broadened and deepened. Antony's eventual defeat in battle by the Roman ruler - and enemy of Cleopatra - Octavius Caesar hastens the tragedy of his death, but our overall sense is that his love affair with Cleopatra was something that could never be contained within this world. Through Enobabrus, Shakespeare not only creates some of his most beautiful lyrics, but provides the famous description of a mesmerising personality:

> *Age cannot wither her, nor custom stale*
> *Her infinite variety: other women cloy*

> *The appetites they feed, but she makes hungry,*
> *Where most she satisfies. For vilest things*
> *Become themselves in her, that the holy priests*
> *Bless her, when she is riggish.*

(II ii 235-8)

Shakespeare was, above all, a pragmatic playwright. His choice of subject matter in *Antony and Cleopatra* may have been in part determined by the fact that contemporary accounts speak of a highly talented boy-actor belonging to the King's Men at this time. *Pericles* (1607/8) also testifies to the practical man of the theatre, in that it shows evidence of being a collaborative work, with the first two acts probably having been penned by somebody else. It would have been extraordinary, given the age's appetite for collaborative pieces (a trend partly instigated by the need for companies to have a constant supply of new works to attract audiences) if Shakespeare had not at some point shared his labour. *Timon of Athens* (*c.*1608?) is another work that bears evidence of shared creation. It is a fascinating, and undeservedly undervalued work, with the depiction of the desertion of the over-generous Timon by his friends, once he falls on hard times, producing one of the bitterest of all Shakespeare's works. Timon comes to believe that the unfettered pursuit of wealth and gold is the root of all social discord:

> *This yellow slave*
> *Will knit and break religions, bless th'accurs'd,*
> *Make the hoar leprosy ador'd, place thieves,*
> *And give them title, knee and approbation*

With senators on the bench. This is it

That makes the wappen'd widow wed again:

She whom the spital-house and ulcerous sores

Would cast the gorge at, this embalms and spices

To th'April day again.

(IV iii 34-42)

This almost Marxist perspective may reflect Shakespeare's concern at the corruption increasingly evident in Jacobean society.

That the playwright himself continued to flourish is confirmed by tax and property records. Although we know that he lived in several residences in London (in the parish of St Helen's Bishopsgate in 1596, in Southwark near the Globe in 1599, in Cripplegate, near St Paul's in 1604 and in Blackfriars, where he purchased a 'dwelling house or tenement with th' appurtances' in 1613), the shrewd entrepreneur continued to invest in Stratford - probably in preparation for his

*Shakespeare's signature
at the bottom of the
1613 Blackfriars
mortgage deed.*

British Library Egerton MS
1787

retirement. In 1605 he made the largest investment that we are aware of when he bought half the interest in the lease of tithes (levies) of 'corn, grain, blade and hay' from Old Stratford, Bishopton, and Welcombe, and the tithes 'of wool, lamb, and other small and privy tithes' from the Stratford parish. By agreeing to pay the vendor, Ralph Habaud, a former sheriff of Warwickshire, £22 a year rent, Shakespeare himself accrued £60 a year net, a shrewd piece of business by anyone's standards.

In 1608 Shakespeare's mother, Mary, died and she may have been the model for the peaceable character of Volumnia in *Coriolanus* (*c*.1608). This work, another Roman play (that focuses on the imperious behaviour of Coriolanus), is probably the last one conceived for initial performance at the Globe, for in 1608 a diplomatic incident was to prepare the way for the final stage of Shakespeare's career.

The Last Plays

George Chapman's *The Conspiracy and Tragedy of Charles, Duke of Byron* in 1608 demonstrated the eternal power of drama to unsettle those in authority. By writing (for the Children of the Queen's Revels) the life of an aristocrat who had been executed for treason against the French king, Henri V, as recently as 1602, Chapman was taking a risk. The French ambassador complained bitterly and the English court was also alarmed since Byron had often been compared to the failed regicide, Essex. An edict was issued forbidding the representation 'of any modern Christian kings' and James I soon after gave an order that 'no play shall be henceforth acted in London'. Royal blessing for drama could also prove a royal curse. Eventually, possibly through the payment of bribes, trusted companies such as the King's Men were permitted to take up their activities again, but a heavy price was paid by the company responsible. The Children of the Queen's Revels were forced to vacate their indoor theatre, the Blackfriars. Their loss was Shakespeare's gain.

During 1608, the shareholders of the King's Men decided to broaden their activity by taking on this second venue. In August 1608 a new lease was made out to Henry Evans (who had been responsible for the Children's performances), Cuthbert Burbage, Richard Burbage, John Heminges, Henry Condell, William Sly and William Shakespeare, and the company now had two very different venues at their disposal. Hard evidence is absent about whether Shakespeare wrote his subsequent works for specific performance in the indoor Blackfriars, but it would be sensible to assume, given the repertory nature of the company, that he wrote works that could be adapted for performance in both theatres. As a practical man of the theatre, Shakespeare had been used to seeing his plays transferred from various theatres to the court throughout his entire career, so moving between the Globe and the Blackfriars would not have been an unfamiliar situation.

For Shakespeare, the experience of watching his works indoors would have been novel. The capacity of the Blackfriars was much smaller, holding fewer than 600 people. The cheapest seats in one of the three galleries were sixpence, with sixpence more required to obtain a stool to perch along the stage. This represented a considerable increase compared with the cost of attending the much larger Globe, and is likely to have attracted a different type of audience. The venue would inevitably have been darker, with natural light allowed through shuttered windows if required, and candlelight from low-hanging candelabra. Do the last plays betray an interest in the potential of different lighting effects, with the light and shadows of *The Tempest* and the 'statue' of Hermione in *The Winter's Tale*?

Cymbeline (c.1609), *The Winter's Tale* (c.1611) and *The Tempest* (c.1611) - generally known, mistakenly, as the 'Last Plays' - all contain a romantic element and a strand of tragi-comedy. Both *The Winter's Tale* and *The Tempest* are among the best loved plays of the canon. In *The Winter's Tale* the story of the schism between Hermione and Leontes, caused by the king's terrifying display of jealousy, explains the chilly nature of the title, but their eventual reconciliation allows the work to be described as a 'romance', with touches of the resolution achieved at the end of earlier comedies, though without the sense of overwhelming joy. *The Tempest*, too, is a work that is enriched by its mixture of genres. It might have been a Revenge Tragedy, with Prospero seeking redress from his usurping brother, Antonio, but he chooses to forgive him:

> *For you, most wicked sir, whom to call a brother*
> *Would even infect my mouth, I do forgive*
> *Thy rankest fault - all of them; and require*
> *My dukedom of thee, which perforce, I know,*
> *Thou must restore.*

(V I 130-4)

Equally, it could have been a study of intellectual hubris, like *Dr Faustus*, with Prospero exploiting his powers for futile or destructive ends. But instead, the magician uses his powers to achieve reconciliation on the magical isle and it may be that this note of harmony, symbolised by the love of Ferdinand and Miranda, signals the middle-aged playwright's new desire for personal contentment. An early performance of *The Tempest* was given at court in 1611. No doubt the king would have appreciated its mix of subdued spirits, benign magic and peaceful resolution.

Retirement

At the end of *The Tempest* Prospero utters his famous speech where he describes all the wondrous spells that he has performed and explains why he has now decided to give up his magic:

> *Ye elves of hills, brooks, standing lakes, and groves;*
> *And ye that on the sand with printless foot*
> *Do chase the ebbing Neptune, and do fly him*
> *When he comes back; you demi-puppets that*
> *By moonshine do the green sour ringlets make,*
> *Whereof the ewe not bites; and you whose pastime*
> *Is to make midnight mushrooms, that rejoice*
> *To hear the solemn curfew; by whose aid -*
> *Weak masters though ye be - I have bedimm'd*
> *The noontide sun, call'd forth the mutinous winds,*
> *And 'twixt the green sea and the azur'd vault*
> *Set roaring war: to the dread rattling thunder*
> *Have I given fire, and rifted Jove's stout oak*
> *With his own bolt; the strong-bas'd promontory*
> *Have I made shake, and by the spurs pluck'd up*
> *The pine and cedar: graves at my command*
> *Have wak'd their sleepers, op'd, and let 'em forth*
> *By my so potent Art.* But this rough magic
> I here abjure; and, when I have requir'd
> Some heavenly music, - which even now I do -
> To work mine end upon their senses, that
> This airy charm is for, I'll break my staff,
> Bury it certain fadoms in the earth,
> And deeper than did ever plummet sound
> I'll drown my book.

(V I 32-57)

Inevitably, it is tempting to read this speech biographically, as if it signals Shakespeare's retirement from the King's Men and the theatre. But although he was now forty-seven, a fine age for a Jacobean gentleman, his career was not quite over. One play, which he probably co-authored with John Fletcher in 1613, *Cardenno*, is now lost, but two, final collaborative pieces survive, *The Famous History of the Life of King Henry the Eighth* (probably known as *All Is True*, 1613, collaborators unknown) and a work now ascribed to Shakespeare and Fletcher, *The Two Noble Kinsmen* (1613). Of all the performances of Shakespeare's plays during his lifetime, the one of *Henry VIII* on 29 June 1613 is the most recorded - because it resulted in the burning down of the Globe. The diplomat, Sir Henry Wotton, supplied an account of this disaster to his nephew in a letter three days later:

> *I will entertain you at the present with what hath happened this week at the Bankside. The King's players had a new play called **All is True**, representing some principal pieces of the reign of Henry VIII, which was set forth with many extraordinary circumstances of pomp and majesty, even to the matting of the stage; the Knights of the Order, with their Georges and Garter, the Guards with their embroidered coats and the like, sufficient in truth within a while to make greatness very familiar, if not ridiculous. Now, King Henry making a masque at the Cardinal Wolsey's house, and certain chambers being shot off at his entry, some of the paper or other stuff wherewith one of them was stopped did light on the thatch, where being thought at first but an idle smoke, and their eyes more attentive to the show, it kindled inwardly and ran round like a train, consuming within less than an hour the whole house to the very grounds. This was the fatal period of that virtuous fabric, wherein yet nothing did perish but wood and straw and a few forsaken cloths; only one man had his breeches set on fire, that would perhaps have broiled him if he had not by the benefit of a provident wit put it out with a bottle of ale.*

Nobody knows whether the Globe fire or general weariness caused Shakespeare to cease writing. The Globe was rebuilt, but its reincarnation did not have the fortune to premiere a new play by the company's most notable writer. He had returned to

Stratford with thoughts of his own mortality, for some time after July 1614 he dictated his will, signing the third and last sheet clearly. The marriage of his daughter, Judith, required some later revisions to it, and the signature on this amended version of 1616 is less sure. The chief beneficiary was his daughter, Susanna, who was to inherit New Place and much of her father's other property. That his wife, Anne, was famously left 'my second-best bed with the furniture' may not indicate strained marital relations. As Schoenbaum has pointed out, under English law, the widow was entitled to inherit a third of the husband's estate as a matter of course.

At the age of fifty-four, Shakespeare died, a very wealthy man. He was buried on 25 April 1616 in the chancel of Holy Trinity Church, Stratford, where he had been a churchwarden. Tradition would claim that he therefore must have died on 23 April, St George's Day. His grave bore a fearsome inscription, designed to ward off grave robbers and prevent the practice of throwing bones from old graves against the chancel wall, as well as to testify to his artistic skill:

> *Good friend for Jesus' sake forbear,*
> *To dig the dust enclosed here!*
> *Blessed be the man that spares these stones,*
> *And cursed be he that moves my bones.*

With Shakespeare's death, the legends began.

❧ 'Not of an age, but for all time'

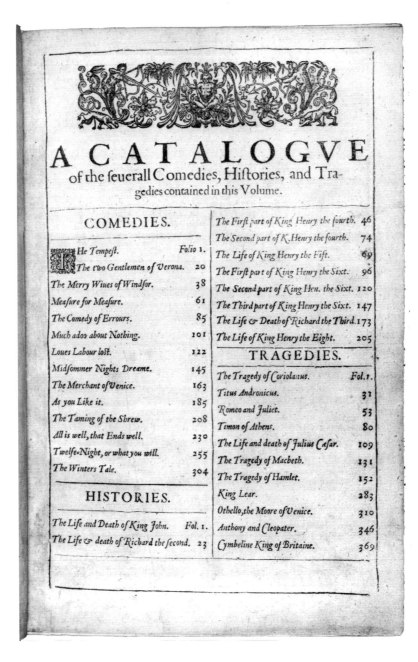

The contents page of
the First Folio.

British Library C.39.k.15

A CATALOGVE
of the seuerall Comedies, Histories, and Tragedies contained in this Volume.

That we have any reliable record at all of Shakespeare's texts is almost entirely due to the labours of two of his colleagues in the King's Men, John Heminges and Henry Condell. During Shakespeare's life-time, individual versions of the plays had been published, but their authenticity was questionable. Eight were produced by unscrupulous printers with perhaps no reference to the playwright's own copy, and these imperfect Bad Quartos included *The Contention*, *The True Tragedy* (both pirated versions related to the *Henry VI* trilogy), *A Shrew*, *Romeo and Juliet*, *Merry Wives of Windsor*, *Henry V*, *Hamlet* and *King John*. Fourteen more reliable texts, which bore some connection to Shakespeare's hand, were also published, but even these Good Quartos should be seen as provisional, unrevised works. They include *Titus Andronicus*, *Love's Labour's Lost*, *Romeo and Juliet*, *Richard II*, *Richard III*, *Henry IV Parts 1 and 2*, *Merchant of Venice*, *Midsummer Night's Dream*, *Much Ado*, *Hamlet*, *Troilus and Cressida*, *King Lear* and *Othello*. The Folio produced in 1623 by Heminges and Condell was the first collected edition of the plays, and although it is not the ultimate authority, the fact that it was compiled by two of Shakespeare's friends, fellow shareholders at the Globe and beneficiaries in his will, means that it has claimed preeminence. In this priceless work, the editors attribute thirty-six plays to Shakespeare's authorship, although they omit two others (*Pericles* and *The Two Noble Kinsmen*) that he is now felt to have had a hand in. In their preliminary remarks they reveal that their intention is 'onely to keep the memory of so worthy a Friend, & Fellow aliue, as was our *Shakespeare*' and they go on to offer to 'the great variety of readers' a condemnation of the earlier versions, a defence of their effort and a most magnificent commendation of their friend and colleague:

> *It had bene a thing, we confesse, worthie to haue bene wished, that the Author himselfe had liu'd to haue set forth, and ouerseen his owne writings; But since it hath bin ordain'd otherwise, and he by death departed from that right, we pray you do not envie his Friends, the office of their care, and paine, to haue collected & publish'd them; and so to haue publish'd them, as where (before) you were abus'd with diuerse stolne, and surreptitious copies, maimed, and deformed by the frauds and stealthes of iniurious imposters, that expos'd them: euen those, are now offer'd to your view cur'd, and perfect of their limbes; and all the rest, absolute in their numbers, as he conceiued them. Who, as he was a happie imitator of Nature, was a most gentle expresser of it. His mind and hand went together: And what he thought, he vttered with that easinesse, that*

wee haue scarse receiued from him a blot in his papers. But it is not our prouince, who onely gather his works, and giue them to you, to praise him. It is yours that reade him. And there we hope, to your diuers capacities, you will find enough, both to draw, and hold you: for his wit can no more lie hid, then it could be lost. Reade him, therefore; againe, and againe: And if then you doe not like him, surely you are in some manifest danger, not to vnderstande him. And so we leaue you to other of his Friends, whom if you need, can bee your guides: if you neede them not, you can leade your selues, and others. And such Readers we wish him.

The prefatory material of the First Folio also contained a poem 'To The Memory of My Beloved, The Author, Mr William Shakespeare' by Ben Jonson, in which the other great playwright of the period generously claimed that Shakespeare 'was not of an age, but for all time'. But how true is this sentiment?

In many ways Shakespeare is very much of his age. His language alone locates him in the Elizabethan and Jacobean era. When in sonnet 130 ('My Mistress eyes are nothing like the sun'), the poet states that

in some perfumes there is more delight
Than in the breath that from my mistress reeks

(7-8)

a modern reader might suppress a snigger at her apparent halitosis, but for an Elizabethan reader the work 'reeks' possessed the more prosaic meaning of exhales.

The plays, too, bear evidence of their time of creation. They were written with specific Elizabethan stage conditions in mind, with sections such as the 'tiring house scenes' testifying to the possibility of concealment that the on-stage pillars afforded. Thus, we have the famous garden scene involving Beatrice and Benedick in *Much Ado About Nothing*, the death of Polonius behind the arras in *Hamlet* and the continual eavesdropping of characters such as Iago. The plays appropriate earlier theatrical traditions, such as the medieval character of the Vice figure that is re-worked as Falstaff in *Henry IV*. There are specific references to contemporary events, including the voyage of the 'wealthy Andrew' - an Elizabethan ship - in *The Merchant of Venice*, or the trial of the equivocating Jesuit priest, Father Garnet, in *Macbeth*. The texts frequently reflect Elizabethan and Jacobean concerns, be it the insecurity of the Tudor throne (the *Henry VI* tetralogy), the fear of a brutal succession after Elizabeth (*Julius Caesar*), the transition from the medieval to the renaissance world (*Hamlet*), the unsettling effect of the gunpowder plot (*Macbeth*) or the era's continual preoccupation with the business of rule and the nature of kingship (*King Lear*). The very difficulty that modern editors have in adjudicating between the Bad Quartos, Good Quartos and First Folio texts also testifies to the complex conditions of publishing that prevailed at the end of the late sixteenth and first part of the seventeenth century.

But, of course, Shakespeare transcends his time as well, and the plays have frequently taken on the hue of the period in which they have been performed. The history of his reception in his own country shows that he has not always been treated with the reverence (some might say overreverence) which he is accorded today. The theatres in England were closed in 1642 on account of the civil war and on their reopening in 1660 Shakespeare's plays were seen as useful raw material that could benefit from a little improvement, rather than passages of holy writ. Therefore, Nahum Tate's famous version of *King Lear*, which originated in 1681 and held sway for over 150 years, sees the Fool omitted, Edgar and Cordelia as lovers and a happy rather than a tragic ending.

Nicholas Rowe's first critical edition of Shakespeare's works in 1709 contained an introduction, entitled *Some Account of the Life, &c, of Mr. William Shakespeare* that is now seen as the first biography, and from this moment on scholarly interest in the playwright began to rise. As the sway of religion began to decline in the eighteenth century and the development of a national identity continued, Shakespeare seemed ideal as a National Poet. Although actors continued to tinker with the plays (strong women, such as Cressida, were sentimentalised and Shylock was permitted to take centre-stage), 'bardolatry' was now taking hold. In 1741 a statue was erected in poet's corner and in 1769 the Garrick Jubilee, a three-day celebration of Shakespeare's life at Stratford organised by the renowned actor, David Garrick, first promoted Stratford as a place of pilgrimage.

The Romantics rediscovered a different Shakespeare by the end of the eighteenth century. They admired the way that he ignored the neo-classical rules for writing plays (unsurprisingly, given that they were formulated after his death) and celebrated the predominance of the heart over the head in his works. The Victorians similarly fashioned him in their own image, viewing him as a repository of universal knowledge and a yardstick against which civilised societies (like their own) could be judged. By the mid-twentieth century, Shakespeare, now a malleable cultural icon, was seen as the quintessential Englishman. He could be used to stiffen national resolve at times of crisis (as in Olivier's morale-boosting film of *Henry V* during the Second World War) or disguise the poverty of modern English theatre in the early 1950s.

The founding of the Royal Shakespeare Company by Peter Hall in 1961 was a vital event in the history of the reception of Shakespeare in Britain. Now possessing three venues at Stratford (the Shakespeare Memorial Theatre, the Swan and The Other Place) and two in London (the Barbican Theatre and The Pit), the RSC, above all other companies, has been responsible for disseminating innovative productions of Shakespeare's plays in a cornucopia of styles, modern and Elizabethan, to generations of school-children, adults and tourists. It has also become a major source of income for the British economy.

Shakespeare's power to sell has been increasingly evident in the last fifty years. Possessing what has become one of the most recognisable faces in the world, in the 1990s alone, the words of John of Gaunt in *Richard II* wrenched out of context ('this happy isle') have been used to sell Typhoo tea, and in Britain both the Labour and the Conservative parties have tried to enlist his support, through his plays, for their cause.

It is perhaps Shakespeare's very elusiveness, the complexity and innovation of his drama, the enormous scope of his wisdom and the fact that we know less than we would like to about his life that guarantees his continual popularity. The fact that he is the only compulsory author on the National Curriculum for British schoolchildren also helps, although compulsion has never guaranteed popularity.

Shakespeare was outlived by his wife and two daughters, although neither of his children were to produce the male heir that would have perpetuated the family name. The death of his granddaughter, Elizabeth, in 1670 marked the end of his direct line, but Shakespeare's enduring heirs are the thirty-eight plays and various poems. Returning to our questioning of Ben Jonson's claim in the First Folio, they are both time-less and time-full. By continuing to reflect the age in which they were created they keep alive a rich and important period of British history and by engaging with the era in which they are received they help to inform us about ourselves and our modern society .

Following pages anti-clockwise from top left:

The Swan Theatre, Stratford-upon-Avon.

John Walker

Film versions of Romeo and Juliet *and* Much Ado About Nothing *have introduced Shakespeare's work to a wider audience.*

British Film Institute

Laurence Olivier as Hamlet.

British Film Institute

Kenneth Branagh and Denzil Washington as Benedick and Don Pedro in Branagh's film of Much Ado About Nothing.

British Film Institute

WILLIAM SHAKESPEARE: 1564-1616

〜 *Chronology*

*c.*1529	John Shakespeare (father) born
1534	Act of Supremacy. Henry VIII becomes the supreme head of the (Protestant) Church of England
1536-40	Dissolution of the monasteries
*c.*1540	Mary Arden (mother) born
1547	Henry VIII dies; Edward VI becomes king
1549	First Protestant Prayer Book introduced as sole form of worship
1552	29 April John Shakespeare fined one shilling for making a dunghill in Henley Street
1553	Edward VI dies; Mary I becomes Queen
*c.*1556	Anne Hathaway (wife) born
1556	17 June Thomas Suche of Armscote seeks to recover £8 from 'Johannem Shakyspeyr...glover'
	24 November Robert Arden (grandfather) leaves 'all my land in Wilmcote, cawlide Asbyes, and the crop apone the grounde sowne and tyllide as hitt is', as well as £6.13*s*.4*d* to his youngest daughter, Mary
*c.*1557	John Shakespeare marries Mary Arden
1557	3 June John Shakespeare, borough ale-taster, fined 8d for his absence
1558	Mary I dies; Elizabeth I becomes Queen
	15 September Joan Shakespeare (sister) christened, presumed to have died in her infancy

30 September John Shakespeare described as a constable in civic records

1 October John Shakespeare serves as a juror

1559   April John Shakespeare and others fined 'for not kepynge their gutteres cleane'

1562   3 October John Shakespeare described as chamberlain (borough treasurer)

2 December Margaret (sister) christened

1563   30 April Margaret buried

1564   24 April William born

26 April William christened

11 July Outbreak of plague claims the lives of some 200 Stratford inhabitants

1565   4 July John Shakespeare appointed an alderman

1566   13 October Gilbert (brother) christened

1568   4 September John Shakespeare elected 'balyf' (mayor) of Stratford

4 November John Shakespeare sells five hundredweight of wool to John Walford of Marlborough

Mary, Queen of Scots, arrives in England

1569   15 April Joan (second sister of that name) christened

1569   John Shakespeare described as a 'Baylife, A Justice of peace, the Queenes officer & cheffe of the towne of Stratford vppon Avon' in an unsuccessful application on his behalf for a coat of arms

c. August the Queen's Players and the Earl of Worcester's Men perform in Stratford

1570	John Shakespeare twice accused of breaking usury laws by making loans of £80 and £100 to Walter Musshem and of charging £20 interest on both loans
	Pope Pius V excommunicates Elizabeth I
1571	September John Shakespeare elected Chief Alderman (Lord Mayor) for the forthcoming year
	28 September Anne (sister) christened
	John Shakespeare fined 40s for illegal wool dealing
1572	Acte for the Punishment of Vacabondes establishes companies with patrons
1573	7 February John Shakespeare briefs the council on his visit to London where he reported on parliamentary matters affecting Stratford
	*c.*September Earl of Leicester's Men, led by James Burbage, perform in Stratford
	John Shakespeare described as 'whyttawer' (dresser of skins and hides) in civic suit
1574	11 March Richard (brother) born
1575	*c.*August Earl of Warwick's Men perform in Stratford
1576	5 September John Shakespeare attends his last council meeting for some years
	James Burbage erects the first permanent playhouse in England, The Theatre
1577	Curtain playhouse erected
1578	29 January John Shakespeare relieved of his duty to finance the maintenance of three pikemen, two billmen and one archer

19 November John Shakespeare relieved of his duty to pay a weekly tax for the poor, levied on aldermen

1579   11 February Lord Strange's Men perform in Stratford

4 April Anne (sister) buried

Easter John Shakespeare mortgages Mary's Asbies property

*c.*August Countess of Essex's Players perform in Stratford

15 October John and Mary Shakespeare's ninth share of her father's property and land sold to Robert Webbe for £4

1580   3 May Edmund (brother) christened

John Shakespeare fined £40 for failing to appear before a London court to promise to keep the peace towards the queen and her subjects

1581   John Shakespeare's Catholic will dictated

Earl of Worcester's Men and Berkeley's Men in Stratford

The Master of the Revels, Edmund Tilney, empowered with the censoring of plays

1582   John Shakespeare petitions for 'sureties of peace against [the bailiff of Stratford] Ralph Cawdrey, William Russell, Thomas Logginge and Robert Young, for fear of death and mutilation of his limbs'

Richard Hathaway (father-in-law) dies

27 November special marriage licence for William Shakespeare and Anne Hathaway granted by the Bishop of Worcester

John Shakespeare present at first council meeting for six years

Berkeley's Men and Lord Chandos's Men perform in Stratford

1583	26 May Susanna (daughter) christened
	Beginning of the 'lost years'
1585	2 February Hamnet and Judith (twin children) christened
1586	6 September John Shakespeare replaced as an alderman having 'not come to the halles when they be warned, nor hathe not done of longe tyme'
1587	Mary, Queen of Scots, executed
	Rose theatre built
1588	John Shakespeare involved in several legal actions
	Defeat of the Spanish Armada
	? The Spanish Tragedy (Thomas Kyd)
1591	*? Dr Faustus* (Christopher Marlowe)
1592	John Shakespeare listed as a recusant
	3 March Henry VI acted by the Admiral's Men takes £3.16*s*.8*d* at the Rose.
	Performances continue until June.
	3 September Robert Greene's *Groats-worth of Witte, bought with a million of Repentance* published (alludes to Shakespeare as 'an vpstart Crow')
	20 September London theatres closed because of plague
	December Henry Chettle, Greene's editor, apologises for the insult to Shakespeare in *Kind-Hart's Dream*
	Titus Andronicus, Romeo and Juliet, The Two Gentlemen of Verona, The Taming of the Shrew, Love's Labour's Lost, A Midsummer Night's Dream, Henry VI (Parts 1, 2 and 3), Richard III and *King John* written by this date
1593	6 January *Titus Andronicus* performed by Strange's Men

2 February to June London theatres closed because of plague

1594	18 April *Venus and Adonis* published

Christopher Marlowe killed in a tavern brawl

? The Comedy of Errors

1594	9 May *The Rape of Lucrece* published

Formation of Lord Chamberlain's Men

1595	15 March Shakespeare named as joint payee with William

Kemp and Richard Burbage for the performance of 'two

several comedies or interludes' given before the queen the

previous Christmas at Greenwich

Swan theatre built

? Richard II

1596	Hamnet (son) dies

? Henry IV Part 1

Shakespeare recorded as living in Bishopsgate

1597	*? Henry IV Part 2*

? The Merchant of Venice

? The Merry Wives of Windsor

Shakespeare purchases New Place, the second largest house
 in Stratford

James I writes *Daemonologie*

1598	Francis Meres' *Wit's Treasury* speaks of the 'sugared

sonnets' circulating amongst Shakespeare's 'private friends'

Shakespeare storing large amounts of grain in his Stratford

barns

? Much Ado About Nothing

Shakespeare acts in Ben Jonson's *Every Man in his Humour*

28 December The Theatre is dismantled and its timbers used to construct the Globe

1599   21 February Lease signed for Globe on the Bankside

? As You Like It

? Julius Caesar

September Thomas Platter records seeing a performance of *Julius Caesar* at the Globe

James I writes *Basilikon Doron*

Shakespeare recorded as living in Southwark near the Globe

1600   The Fortune theatre is built

? Hamlet

? Twelfth Night

1601   7 February Lord Chamberlain's Men commissioned to perform *Richard II* at the Globe

8 February Earl of Essex launches his abortive rebellion against Elizabeth I

John Shakespeare dies

1602   *? Troilus and Cressida*

1 May Shakespeare pays £320 for 107 acres of arable land in Old Stratford

John Manningham records the Richard III/William the Conqueror anecdote

1603   19 March Theatres closed as mark of respect for the dying queen

24 March Elizabeth I dies; James I becomes king

Shakespeare performs in Ben Jonson's *Sejanus His Fall*

19 May letters patent announce that the Lord Chamberlain's Men will become the King's Men

26 May theatres close for eleven months because of virulent

plague which kills almost 30,000 Londoners

? All's Well That Ends Well

1604　James I ends wars with Spain - King's Men perform for

Spanish Ambassador at Somerset House

Hampton Court Conference on religion

? Measure for Measure

? Othello

Shakespeare recorded living in Cripplegate,

near St Paul's

1605　*? King Lear*

5 November Intended date of assassination of James I by

Gunpowder plotters

Shakespeare makes his largest recorded purchase, of tithes

in Stratford

1606　*? Macbeth*

1607　Edmund (brother) dies

? Antony and Cleopatra

? Pericles

1608　*? Timon of Athens*

August King's Men take out a lease on the Blackfriars

indoor theatre

1609　*? Cymbeline*

1611　Publication of King James Bible

? The Winter's Tale

? The Tempest

1612　Gilbert (brother) dies

1613　Richard (brother) dies

? Cardenno, co-authored with John Fletcher, now lost

? Henry VIII

29 June the Globe burns down during a performance of *Henry VIII*

Shakespeare buys a 'dwelling house or tenement with th' appurtances' in Blackfriars

1614   Shakespeare dictates will

1616   Judith Shakespeare marries Thomas Quiney

Shakespeare revises will

?23 April Shakespeare dies

25 April Shakespeare buried in Holy Trinity Church, Stratford

1623   John Heminges and Henry Condell produce the First Folio

1646   Joan (sister) dies

1649   Susanna (daughter) dies

1662   Judith (daughter) dies

1670   Elizabeth (granddaughter) dies. Direct line ends

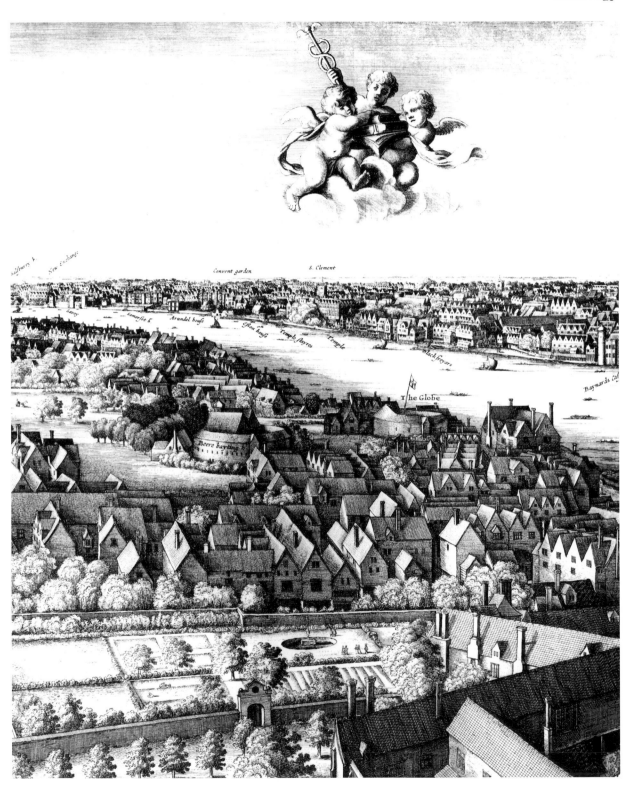

To the Reader.

This Figure, that thou here seeſt put,
    It was for gentle Shakeſpeare cut;
VVherein the Grauer had a ſtrife
    with Nature, to out-doo the life :
O, could he but haue drawne his wit
    As well in braſſe, as he hath hit
Hisface , the Print would then ſurpaſſe
    All, that vvas euer vvrit in braſſe.
But, ſince he cannot, Reader, looke
    Not on his Picture, but his Booke.

                              B. I.

Mr. WILLIAM
SHAKESPEARES

COMEDIES,
HISTORIES, &
TRAGEDIES.

Published according to the True Originall Copies.

Martin Droeshout sculpsit London.

LONDON

Printed by Isaac Iaggard, and Ed. Blount. 1623.

Further Reading

Andrew Gurr
The Shakespearean Stage 1574-1642
Cambridge University Press, 1992

John Guy
Tudor England
Oxford University Press, 1990

ed. J.R.Mulryne and Margaret Shewring
Shakespeare's Globe Rebuilt
Cambridge University Press, 1997

Eric Sams
The Real Shakespeare: Retrieving the Early Years 1564-94
Yale University Press, 1995

S. Schoenbaum
Shakespeare's Lives
Oxford University Press, 1991

Peter Thomson
Shakespeare's Theatre
Routledge, 1994

Simon Trussler
The Cambridge Illustrated History of British Theatre
Cambridge University Press, 1994

Stanley Wells
Shakespeare: A Dramatic Life
Sinclair-Stevenson, 1994

 # Index

Front cover:
Portrait of Shakespeare, engraved by Martin Droeshout, on the title-page of the First Folio of Shakespeare's works *(British Library C.39.k.15)*
Manuscript of a contribution to *The Play of Sir Thomas More*, thought to be in Shakespeare's own hand *(British Library Harley MS 7368, f.9)*
Wenceslas Hollar's *Long View of London* (1644). The captions on the Globe Theatre and the Hope bear-baiting house were reversed *(Guildhall Library)*

Back cover:
Portrait of Elizabeth I taken from a Guild Book of the Barber Surgeons in York
(British Library)
The Birthplace *(John Walker)*

Half-title page:
Portrait of Shakespeare attributed to John Taylor (died 1651) *(National Portrait Gallery)*

Frontispiece:
Portrait of Shakespeare, engraved by Martin Droeshout, on the title-page of the First Folio of Shakespeare's works, 1623 *(British Library C.39.k.15)*

Contents spread:
View of the Thames. Detail from Claes Janz, Visscher's London (Amsterdam, 1616).
(British Library Maps C.5.a.6)

Photographic acknowledgements:

The British Library is grateful to the following for permission to reproduce illustrations:
The British Film Institute; the Fellows of Corpus Christi College, Cambridge; the Trustees of Dulwich Picture Gallery; the Marquis of Bath; Guildhall Library; John Walker; the Fellows of Magdalen College, Cambridge; Shakespeare's Globe; The Society of Antiquaries; The Trustees of the National Portrait Gallery; Utrecht University Library; The Trustees of the Victoria and Albert Museum.

Published in the United States of America by
Oxford University Press, Inc.
198 Madison Avenue
New York, NY 10016
Oxford is a registered trademark of Oxford University Press, Inc.
First published in paperback in 2000

ISBN 0-19-521442-0 lib. ed.   ISBN 0-19-521655-5 paperback ed.

First published 1998 by The British Library, 96 Euston Road, London NW1 2DB

Designed and typeset by Crayon Design, Stoke Row, Henley-on-Thames
Printed in Italy by Artegrafica